MOTHERS OF RETARDED CHILDREN

CHILDREN

How They Feel; Where They Find Help

MOTHERS OF RETARDED CHILDREN

How They Feel; Where They Find Help

By

WALTER H. EHLERS, D.S.W.

Professor of Social Work
Florida State University
Tallahassee, Florida

With a Foreword by

Dorothy Garst Murray

CHARLES C THOMAS • **PUBLISHER**
Springfield · Illinois · U.S.A.

Published and Distributed Throughout the World by
CHARLES C THOMAS • PUBLISHER
BANNERSTONE HOUSE
301-327 East Lawrence Avenue, Springfield, Illinois, U.S.A.
NATCHEZ PLANTATION HOUSE
735 North Atlantic Boulevard, Fort Lauderdale, Florida, U.S.A.

With THOMAS BOOKS careful attention is given to all details of manufacturing and design. It is the Publisher's desire to present books that are satisfactory as to their physical qualities and artistic possibilities and appropriate for their particular use. THOMAS BOOKS will be true to those laws of quality that assure a good name and good will.

Printed in the United States of America
W-2

DEDICATION

To the mothers who helped make this study possible and to all mothers of the retarded everywhere.

FOREWORD

Someone has sagely observed that "an ounce of demonstration is worth a ton of speculation." Those of us who can accept this observation as a valid one can wholeheartedly endorse Dr. Walter H. Ehlers' *Mothers of Retarded Children* as being an invaluable addition to the growing amount of literature which is now being produced for the purpose of developing and improving services in behalf of the mentally retarded. For Dr. Ehlers has turned his back on theoretical speculation and has made an effort to find out what services are most needed and most valuable by seeking the advice and help of those who, of all persons, are most vitally concerned with this problem—the mothers of the mentally retarded. It is the mothers of mentally retarded children who, in the final analysis, bear the brunt of the burden for their care and training. In the face of this very obvious fact, it is interesting and also regrettable that not until now has serious research been undertaken concerning the type of help which mothers most sorely need in acquiring more competence and security in the day-by-day management of the multitude of problems which they face. It would appear that in past years many services for the retarded may have been established on the basis of what the professional disciplines believed their needs to be rather than upon what the families themselves see as their basic needs. If this book serves as a stimulus toward further exploratory research into cooperation between the families of the retarded and the various professional disciplines in the evaluation of services, it will indeed fill a real need.

It is a difficult feat to take statistical information acquired through research and present it in such a manner that it is both interesting and stimulating. That Dr. Ehlers has succeeded in doing this is not only a tribute to his ability as a writer but to his carefulness and honesty as a researcher. To the person who is sincerely interested in the welfare of the retarded the results of this study will not only prove interesting, but will challenge the individual to try just a little harder to improve his own personal contribution to the welfare of the retarded.

I believe there are a number of professional disciplines that will benefit from a careful consideration of the material presented in this book. The thoughtful social worker and psychologist will want to know why mothers of the retarded appear to have some reservations about the real value of their roles as a "helping" profession. Is it because these two professions are relative newcomers in comparison with the older and more established professions such as public health nursing and medicine? Could it be that mothers may have an unconscious resentment against the social caseworker or psychologist because they must sometimes help the mother to see herself as she *really* is and not as she *thinks* herself to be? Self-evaluation is nearly always a painful process and those individuals who have the capacity for helping us to ferret out our weak spots arc not likely to be eagerly sought after in any case! Perhaps this may be the reason many mothers expressed genuine appreciation for the relief they felt in being able to talk with the public health nurses in their own homes on a regular basis, yet felt quite positively that "going to the office and talking with a social worker isn't going to help you." Do mothers see the caseworkers as posing so much of a threat to their egos that they just aren't quite comfortable in their presence? These are some of the many questions which need further study in light of some of the facts which were uncovered by Dr. Ehlers' research.

Perhaps the most valuable contribution of the book to all professional disciplines is the challenge in Chapter V to work toward developing a more effective team concept in the clinics and other areas where various disciplines are working with the parents for the benefit of the child. Dr. Ehlers makes a frank and forthright evaluation of why the team concept sometimes fails. This evaluation deserves the thoughtful consideration of every professional person who works with and for the mentally retarded. Speaking as a mother and as a "consumer of the service,"

I feel compelled to say that probably no one factor does so much real harm to the security and well-being of parents, and thus indirectly to the retardate, as the all too obvious conflicts which too often exist among those professional persons whose avowed intent is to promote the welfare of the retarded.

Mothers of Retarded Children will have a different meaning and fulfill a different need for a broad spectrum of persons. For the physician it will provide some enlightenment as to *what, when, why,* and *how* parents should be told about mental retardation in their children with the least emotional damage to the parent and consequently the greatest good to the child. Members of clinic teams and other professional persons will, we believe, be stimulated by this book to the kind of self-examination which will enable them to see their individual contributions with greater objectivity. Members of Associations for Retarded Children will discover here the necessity for a re-evaluation of their own efforts in order to be sure that they are indeed serving the parents of "all retarded children, wherever they may be" and not just a certain segment or class of parents. Clergymen of every faith will no doubt be startled (and they should be!) by the discovery that mothers do not go to their clergymen when they begin to seek help for their retarded children. Sociologists, welfare workers, educators, governmental officials at local, state and national levels —all who are directly or indirectly involved in future planning for the needs of the retarded—will find a wealth of useful information in Chapters VIII and IX. Here in clear cut and succinct language Dr. Ehlers has given an overview of the work of the President's Panel on Mental Retardation and a brief resume of the valuable contributions of the Panel's individual Task Forces. The necessity for coordination of services at a local, state and national level is emphasized and some concrete examples of how this is being accomplished in several areas is included.

It is our belief that *Mothers of Retarded Children* may well prove to be a sharp and stimulating tool for use in further chipping away at the mountains of misinformation and misconception and ignorance which for centuries have stood in the way of progressive action in behalf of the mentally retarded. If this proves to be true, perhaps it will be in part because the vast numbers of people involved in providing services had the humility to say at one time or another (with apologies to Robert Burns, of course):

> *"O, wauld had God*
> *Th' giftie gie us*
> *To see ourselves*
> *As* MITHERS *see us—*
> *'Twould from many a blunder free us*
> *And foolish notion!"*

DOROTHY GARST MURRAY

INTRODUCTION

T his book is the result of a study in depth of twenty-four mothers of mentally retarded children, conducted in the Cambridge Service for Retarded Children,[1] Department of Public Health, Cambridge, Massachusetts, and completed by June, 1961. The study sought to discover how the mothers learned that their children were retarded, and how they went about seeking help.

The first chapters describe the research problem, explain why it was selected, discuss the method used in obtaining the information, and in some detail, the effect that such a child has on the family in which he lives. Since somewhere between 18 and 20 million people are members of families with a retarded person, the need for greater attention to these families, and specialized training for the helping professions who work with their children is evident.

The cooperation of the mothers in this study was extremely helpful to the writer. They were eager to talk about their problems and to make suggestions. They seemed to feel, in some cases, and frankly said so in others, that if the study contributed in any way to reducing some of the pain that parents suffer as a result of having a retarded child, they were happy to cooperate. They willingly discussed the services of the clinic, and their reactions to the professionals who helped them with their children.

The CSRC was genuinely interested in having such a study made. They saw the findings as being of possible importance in guiding their programming and administration. The clinic provides diagnostic evaluation and treatment services, and in this

---

[1] Hereafter abbreviated to CSRC. The name of this agency was changed on September 1, 1961, to Children's Developmental Clinic.

respect is similar to more than 139 clinics in the United States now giving special services to the retarded.[2] In the case of the CSRC, there is the additional component of being research oriented under the direction of a study director.[3] All programs of service and research are therefore geared to developing more knowledge in the field of retardation.

Recommendations and implications were drawn from the mothers' responses. The writer hopes they will be in some measure of help to many kinds of people—the social caseworker, the public health nurse, the physician, associations of parents, the clergy, foster home and cottage parents, and clinics serving the mentally retarded and their families.

In addition to the original study, the writer has added, in Chapters VIII and IX, up-to-date material describing "significant services now available," and "prospects for the future." Hopefully, the added material will make this a more useful book for parents, students and professionals working with retarded children and their mothers.

Credit for a great many of the services now available stems from the impetus of the late President Kennedy's dynamic forceful interest and his creation of The President's Panel on Mental Retardation under the able leadership of Leonard W. Mayo, who has an honorary S.Sc.D., as chairman, and George Tarjan, M.D., as vice-chairman.

The results of the Panel's Task Forces are detailed in the report submitted to President Kennedy on October 16, 1962.[4] The resulting legislative action and programs are discussed in Chapter VIII, thereby making available for the present reader a quick overview of the more significant current services.

Prospects for the Future, Chapter IX, was added because it

---

[2] Ida Axelrod, Consultant on Public Health and Nursing, National Association for Retarded Children, 420 Lexington Avenue, New York City, July, 1965.

[3] The study director at the time was Simon Olshansky, whose writings in the field of mental retardation and rehabilitation are extensive. The CSRC also had a clinical director, an M.D.

[4] The President's Panel on Mental Retardation, *A Proposed Program for National Action to Combat Mental Retardation,* U. S. Government Printing Office, Washington, D. C., 1962.

seems to the writer that we can never afford complacency. The pendulum has swung from the quadrant of disinterest as a result of President Kennedy's push in the direction of active concern. While that concern is still strong as of this moment, no one can rest assured that it will remain so. For parents there is a great deal of hope, especially in the light of the federal government's interest and the appropriation of considerable research money. What are the next steps? What still needs to be done and by whom is discussed in Chapter IX. Hopefully this material will provide some guides for the future.

W. H. EHLERS

ACKNOWLEDGMENTS

ONE OF THE realities of life which gets through to us sooner or later regardless of our image of self-sufficiency is the reality of our indebtedness to others. Nowhere is this more apparent than in the field of writing, where debt is recognized in every quotation and every reference. But the sharing of ideas which stimulated new concepts may have come through conversations with colleagues. These debts are hereby recognized although it is not possible to acknowledge all of those who helped in this way—they themselves know of their help and appreciation is expressed in this statement.

Special thanks needs to go to those who gave more than a little bit of their time to making this study possible: Charles I. Schottland, Dean of the Florence Heller Graduate School for Advanced Studies in Social Welfare, Brandeis University for his encouragement and help; to Robert Morris and David G. French of the Florence Heller School faculty; to Leon Sternfeld, M.D., Health Commissioner for the City of Cambridge, Massachusetts during the time of the study[1] and without whose help the work would not have been possible; and to Simon Olshansky, formerly Study Director of the Cambridge Service for Retarded Children[2] who along with his staff and members of the health department made it possible for me to learn a great deal in a very short time about the problems of mothers with retarded children.

My thanks also to Malcolm J. Farrell, M.D., Superintendent

---

[1] Now Director, Division of Local Health Services, Department of Public Health, The Commonwealth of Massachusetts.

[2] Now Director, Community Workshops, Boston.

of the Walter E. Fernald State School who made possible my examination of the school records; to members of his Social Service staff and other staff members who willingly took time to help me and to answer dozens of important questions about the families of the retarded.

I am deeply grateful to Michael J. Begab, Specialist on Social Services to Mentally Retarded Children, U. S. Children's Bureau, and to Howard R. Kelman, Assistant Professor, Departments of Physical Medicine and Rehabilitation and Preventive Medicine, New York Medical College, Metropolitan Medical Center, both of whom read the original study proposal and offered many valuable suggestions; and to Louise M. Noble, Regional Child Welfare Representative, U. S. Children's Bureau, who made available a great deal of material on retardation and took time to discuss various aspects of the problem.

For his help in clarifying many obscure points and smoothing out some of the research problems I acknowledge my debt to Howard E. Freeman, faculty advisor, researcher and friend. His incisive analysis, depth of research knowledge combined with good common sense appraisals of what was being said helped me avoid a number of pitfalls. Whatever mistakes still exist must be counted as my own having crept in after the usual labors of writing and re-writing.

The addition of the last two chapters to the previously written study material has increased my indebtedness to another group—the executive and staff at the National Association for Retarded Children. Library facilities, staff time and discussions with various board members made possible a better understanding of what is going on in the field which is helpful to both mothers and fathers of the retarded, and specifically what is being done by state and national government agencies.

Luther W. Stringham, Executive Director, was kind enough to take time to explain the prime objectives of the National Association which were then filled in specifically in terms of community programs by Curtis H. Krishef, Director, Department of Community Services.[3]

---

[3] Now Instructor, School of Social Welfare, Florida State University.

To my wife Sabine whose help in editing, proofing and indexing made the book readable and whose encouragement made it possible—I owe my deepest appreciation.

W. H. E.

CONTENTS

APPENDIX

TABLES

MOTHERS OF RETARDED CHILDREN

How They Feel; Where They Find Help

Chapter I

THE RESEARCH PROBLEM

Since "mental retardation" is not a clinical entity and the terms mental retardation, mental defect, mental deficiency, and mental subnormality are often used synonymously, it was necessary to be more precise about the sample being selected for study. Thus, the author ruled out culturally or socially defined retardation and selected only cases of clear-cut central nervous system pathology. The sample selected, therefore, was of children about whom there could be little question of retardation by reason of brain damage due to those factors which produce anatomical or chemical abnormalities of the central nervous system. For purposes of this study then, all twenty-four mothers interviewed had children diagnosed by the clinic as brain damaged. In addition, for reasons of comparability, all children selected had an IQ of 50 or less and were under ten years of age.

The research problem therefore centered around how mothers of these children perceived the abnormality; what their decision-making processes were regarding the seeking and using of services; and how they used, responded to, and valued the services rendered.

The questions directed to the mothers attempted to answer the following: Are there differential patterns of reaction associated with the initial observation of mental retardation? What are the subsequent patterns of seeking and using of services? Does a pattern evolve which hopefully might lead us to earlier case finding? Do the mothers of mentally retarded children recognize the child's problems at an early age? At

3

what age do they recognize the problem as one of mental retardation? What do they do about it?

The question of how early the mother perceived the problem of retardation was seen as rather central to the study. It has been proven that early case finding is crucial if proper care and treatment is to be given the retardate so as to result in the optimum functioning possible considering the disability.

It is generally agreed in the field that early diagnosis is important if the family is to be spared years of uncertainty in respect to a possible diagnosis of retardation. What did the mothers do when they were faced with this diagnosis and what did they do about seeking help for themselves as well? We also wanted to know about the mothers' first reactions so that clinics might be in a better position to devise ways of dealing with the various problems of shock, disbelief, guilt, and other family and personal trauma.

RESEARCH QUESTIONS

In the broad area of the problem under study, five research questions were formulated as follows:

(a) What in the child's behavior caused the parents to suspect mental retardation?

(b) What types of persons have conspicuous influence on the parents bringing (or not bringing) the child to an agency giving service to the mentally retarded?

(c) What services were offered and rendered by a specialized community agency for mentally retarded children and their families?

(d) What services were used by the families?

(e) What services did parents report as alleviating or modifying the problems they faced by having a mentally retarded child in the family?

More specifically, the first of the above five questions was aimed at an investigation into the symptons or conditions (e.g., inability to walk, talk, feed self) which the mothers reported as indicating to them the possibility of subnormality. What were the specific indicators which finally led the mothers to this suspicion? How long did they wait from the time of this observation until they brought the child to an agency giving services to the retarded? Were there differential patterns which distinguished the way various families handled this problem?

For the second question, data was gathered from parents about the types of persons from whom they received advice, counsel, and information. "Types of persons" included household members, other relatives, friends, acquaintances, clergy, physicians and other professionals. The subquestions investigated were as follows: what type of persons did the families perceive as having influenced them to go to an agency for retarded children; which persons were reported as being most influential; which persons were reported as being or not being helpful.

The third question relates to the services offered by the agency. What specific services were recommended and which were rendered? Recommended and rendered services for the child, for example, included educational, medical diagnosis, medical treatment, recreational, home training, nutritional, social casework, and psychotherapy; and for the family, diagnostic interpretation, financial aid, housing, recreation, nutrition, psychiatry, and medical aid.

The fourth question deals with the services which mothers accepted and used. Subquestions included the following: Which services did the family want and accept? Which did they reject? What services did they report as wanting which were not available?

The fifth question attempts to identify the mothers' reactions to the services which they say were or were not rendered. Subquestions included the following: Do the parents have their own conflicts and anxieties which they report were alleviated or modified?[1] What about the problem of concrete guidance given the parents so that they could administer to the daily needs of the child?[2] If toilet-training was a specific problem, did the mothers feel that the services rendered helped them to better cope with it? If the problem was one of speech, what services did the mothers ask for and receive?

----

[1] Michael J. Begab: Unmet needs of the mentally retarded in the community. *Amer J Men Defic*, No. 4 62:714, January, 1958.
[2] *Ibid.*

The responses of the mothers, the findings from the case records, and the replies of the staff were compared for the degree of consensus on the five major questions and related subquestions.

ELEMENTS IN RESEARCH

Patterns. Studying the behavior of human beings would be difficult indeed if it were not for the fact that patterns of action and reaction are normally distinguishable. The observation of these patterns then makes it possible for us to be scientific in the sense that it makes it possible for us to predict behavior.[3]

Variables. After we ascertain what the normal or consistent patterns of behavior are then the next question we must ask ourselves is to what degree these patterns differ in respect to any given set of variables. For example, is there a difference which may be accounted for by social class, religion, ethnic background, number of children in the family, birth order, health of the mother, father, and siblings, and age and education of the mother.

Social class: As one of the most important of the variables it is worth examining in more detail. It has been established that services rendered differ along class lines,[4] that behavior patterns differ from one social class to another,[5] that professionals of a middle class orientation may have difficulty accepting the behavior of lower-class working people,[6] and that there is a tendency for the working-class man to find it difficult to function as an individual responsible for his own destiny, that traditionally he is oriented toward authority figures and to those with whom he has already established some relationship.[7]

---

[3] Ely Chinoy, *Sociological Perspective.* New York, Random House, 1954, p. 9.

[4] August B. Hollingshead and Frederick C. Redlich: *Social Class and Mental Illness.* New York, John Wiley and Sons, Inc., 1958, pp. 274-275.

[5] Walter B. Miller: Implications of urban lower class culture. *The Social Service Review*, No. 2, 33:221, September, 1959.

[6] Ibid.

[7] Norman Bell, Albert Trieschman, and Ezra Vogel: "A Sociocultural Analysis of the Resistances of Working-Class Fathers Treated in a Child Psychiatric Clinic." (A mimeographed copy made available through Norman Bell, McLean Hospital, Waverly, Massachusetts, 1959, p. 28.)

From these and other writers who have studied various aspects of class influences[8] a basis was established for the examination of social class factors which would reveal clues useful in programming clinics, for giving services to retardates and their families and for clinic administration.

Religion: Regarding this variable it was necessary to find out if mothers of differing religious persuasions followed differing patterns of behavior. Did the mother turn to the church, that is to the minister or priest, for help and guidance and did she think of the church as a place to look for help in the initial or later stages of concern about possible retardation? What did mothers say about the clergy, the church, or religion in general as to the impact it may have had on them in respect to their retarded child?

Ethnic differences: Another question which needed answering was whether or not persons of similar cultural and environmental backgrounds tended to think alike about their retarded child. In other words, was there an accepted way of treating the child which was looked upon as "right" by a particular ethnic group? If the answer were found to be positive how would the agency rendering service need to take this factor into account? Since social work often has as its goal the changing of customary patterns of behavior, it becomes vital to the profession to know what the patterns are that may vary from one to another ethnic group. Using the same techniques in all cases might be seriously damaging, not only to the client but also to the work of the professional.

Family size: The size of the family was seen as a possibly important variable that might influence the mother's care, treatment, and seeking of help for her retarded child. In a large family would the other children accept the retarded one? Would they help or hinder the care and treatment? Would the mother's

---

[8] See: Melvin L. Kohn: Social class and parental values. *Amer J Sociol* 64:337-351, 1959. Bernard Farber: Perceptions of crisis and related variables—the impact of a retarded child on the mother. *J Health Hum Behav.* No. 1:110 Summer, 1960. Charles V. Willie: The social class of patients that public health nurses prefer to serve. *Amer J Public Health*, No. 8, Vol. 50, August, 1960.

physical condition in caring for a large family make any significant difference in her handling of the retardate?

Birth order: This variable is related to the family size variable and needs to be examined in regard to any possible effect on the mother. Bernard Farber calls attention to the part played by birth order in the care and treatment received by the retardate in that customarily the parents seem to expect their normal child to accept more responsibilities and act in a mature manner, especially towards the retardate. It is further assumed that there might be a difference in the attention received or the emphasis on the retardate depending on where he is in the birth order.[9]

Health: The health of the mother, father, and siblings was of concern in this study for its possible effect on the mother's perceptions and utilization of services. Does a mother who is ill or who has a family in which there is a lot of illness tend to treat her retarded child differently? Is it possible to separate the general complaints of tiredness and nervousness from somatic illness on the part of the mother or the father? Any conditions of ill health, then, must be taken into account for whatever possible effect they may have on the mother's care and treatment of the retarded child.

Age and education: The possible effect of age and education of the mother as it relates to her handling of the retardate was also of concern to this study. Are younger mothers better able to cope? If they in addition happen not to have gone beyond the eighth grade does this make any significant difference? Would an older mother with a high school or college education handle her child differently? What about attitudes as reported by the mothers, do they differ according to age and education? In a study of attitudes toward mental illness, Howard Freeman concluded that education was a crucial variable.[10]

FOUR ELEMENTS IMPORTANT TO CLINICS

The seven variables just discussed are important to the re-

---

[9] Bernard Farber: *Effects of a Severely Mentally Retarded Child on Family Integration*, Monograph, Society for Research in Child Development, Serial No. 71, No. 2, Vol. 23, 1959, pp. 13-14.

[10] Howard E. Freeman: Attitudes toward mental illness among relatives of former patients. *Amer Sociol Rev*, No. 1, 26:59-60, February, 1961.

search problem in terms of understanding the client and the client-clinic relationship. In addition there are four elements of the research problem of crucial importance to understanding the role and function of the clinic giving services to the retarded. They are as follows: (a) the mechanism of early discovery; (b) the help-seeking or "decision-making" process; (c) programming or planning clinical services, and (d) staff consensus.

Early Discovery. Specialists in the field have agreed almost without exception on the need for the earliest possible case finding.[11] Proper care for the retardate at the earliest possible age in clinical programs adequately staffed with a variety of competent personnel will reduce a host of serious problems that would otherwise arise.[12]

What was the pattern of early discovery? How did the mothers generally make the discovery? How soon did they act on the hunch, suggestion, or diagnosis of retardation? How soon did they seek medical advice? Did advice from friends, relatives, or others help or hinder in making an early discovery or not?

The Help-seeking or "Decision-making" Process. This is the phase in which the applicant decides in some way that he is in need of services. The assumption was made that in respect to seeking services for her retarded child a mother would tend to follow a series of steps which could be also described as a pattern.[13]

One possible pattern might be to talk with neighbors, friends, relatives, or clergy attempting to use what has been called a "lay referral"[14] system as a way of getting reactions and suggestions

---

[11] Stanley Powell Davies, *The Mentally Retarded in Society.* New York, Columbia University Press, 1959, p. 179; Rudolf P. Hormuth: The problem of mental retardation. *Public Health News,* 41:287, September, 1960.

[12] World Health Organization: *The Mentally Subnormal Child.* World Health Organization Technical Report Series, No. 75, 1954.

[13] See also David Landy: "Problems of the Person Seeking Help in Our Culture." *The Social Welfare Forum, 1960,* New York, Columbia University Press, 1960; Betty V. Graliker, Arthur H. Parmalee, Sr., and Richard Koch: Attitude study of parents of mentally retarded children. *Pediatrics,* No. 5, Vol. 24, November, 1959. John A. Clausen and Marion Radke Yarrow: Paths to the mental hospital. *The Journal of Social Issues,* No. 4, Vol. 11, 1955; Eliot Freidson: Specialties without roots: the utilization of new services. *Human Organization,* No. 3, Vol. 18.

[14] Friedson, *op. cit.*

regarding what to do about services or help. Another possible pattern would be to avoid the lay referral system and instead go directly to professional medical services. A third pattern might be not to discuss or acknowledge having a retarded child but instead attempt to shield the family and the child from any diagnosis, treatment, or care. Each of these patterns was examined and the possibility of additional patterns was considered.

Programming or Planning Clinical Services. The relative newness of the community clinic concept as a way of giving services to the retarded is the reason that programs and planning are still in need of discussion. This study proceeded on the assumption that one might do well to ask parents of retarded children what they think is needed.[15] The dangers inherent in this procedure are that parents may be emotionally upset at the time of the interview, they may have had some disagreeable news recently from a physician or other clinic member or may be upset because of their intense feelings of frustration, hostility, guilt or aggressiveness (or conversely), their feelings of hopelessness, apathy, or resignation, may inadvertently mislead the interviewer.[16]

Another aspect of the researcher's problem was the necessity of hearing what the mothers said about their needs, and realizing that although they may have come to the clinic for diagnostic evaluation of their child, they undoubtedly also came because they needed understanding, sympathy, and direction.[17] The interviewer then had to listen carefully to the mother's expressed needs and separate her needs from the needs of the child. This kind of information would be crucial to clinic programming, especially since many clinics have been planned only around giving service to the retarded child. The larger picture of the family unit and what having a retarded child does to the family may well call for a restructuring of clinical programs so as to focus on the family.[18]

---

[15] Elizabeth Boggs: State programming for the mentally deficient. *Community Organization,* 1958, New York, Columbia University Press, 1958, pp. 138-139.

[16] Robert M. Nadal: A counseling program for parents of severely retarded pre-school children. *Social Casework,* No. 2, 62:80, February, 1961.

[17] Abraham Levinson and John A. Bigler: *Mental Retardation in Infants and Children.* Chicago, The Yearbook Publishers, Inc., 1960, p. 12.

The problem then for this study was to find out whatever we could that would be helpful in clinic programming. What more is needed besides diagnostic evaluation? Begab has suggested that for one thing the function of the social worker and of the other staff members should be considered in greater detail.[19] Hormuth says that there is:

> . . . ample evidence that many parents request placement because there is no help available through existing community programs. Given good pediatric services, including help in home training and activities of daily living, many of the parents no longer see the need for placement.[20]

A study by Tizard in London indicates in reference to the problems of the parents "the need for more integration in the general maternal and child welfare services and in the social welfare services for other handicapped persons."[21] Supporting documentation of this concept is found in the report by the Group for the Advancement of Psychiatry where they say

> Diagnostic facilities function most effectively if they are integral parts of the health, education and welfare structures of the community. The offices of private physicians and the clinics of both general and specialized hospitals must be prepared to initiate this type of service. A multi-discipline approach is essential, involving the participation of the pediatrician, neurologist, psychiatrist, social worker and psychologist as well as the public health nurse, the educator, and others as required.[22]

---

[18] The CSRC program did have as its goal working with the entire family, so mothers were considered in the total treatment plan. For more complete description of the Cambridge Health Department program for retarded children see *Edward Wellin et al.*, Community aspects of mental subnormality—A local health department program for retarded children. *Amer J Public Health*. No. 1, Vol. 50, January, 1960.

[19] Michael Begab, *op. cit.*

[20] Rudolf Hormuth, *The Public Health Nurse in Community Planning for the Mentally Retarded.* Washington, U. S. Department of Health, Education, and Welfare, 1957, p. 10.

[21] J. Tizard, Public health aspects of severe mental subnormality. *Roy Soc Health J*, No. 4, 80:331, July-August, 1960.

[22] *Report No. 43, Basic Considerations in Mental Retardation: A Preliminary Report*, New York, Group for the Advancement of Psychiatry, 1959, p. 20.

The foregoing statements regarding the broader needs of the family were therefore taken into account in studying what the mothers had to say. The results of the interviews and the implications for the various professional disciplines and agencies may be found in the later chapters of this book

Staff Consensus. As mentioned earlier most of the new thinking is in the direction of multi-disciplinary services with a team of workers giving a variety of services. In many respects this plan of rendering multiple services through one facility makes a great deal of sense. Administratively, however, it often proves to be difficult. Professional jealousies, differences in training, background or experience, even differences in philosophical approaches to the patient may result in something less than adequate services or a treatment plan which turns out to be a poor compromise.

The team approach then, being a relatively new concept, needed examination in a study such as this so that certain strengths and weaknesses may be identified. One question felt to be of particular importance was whether or not treatment and services were affected adversely by lack of consensus. The functions of the public health nurse and the social worker may overlap at a number of points.[23] Might this result in differences of professional approach detrimental to the patient? Similarly the psychiatrist or the psychologist and the physician may have differing diagnoses. One treatment plan, however, is finally agreed upon. Can both professionals overcome their differences so as to give the plan a fair trial? Is this a personal matter? Are there patterns that certain professionals follow? Can satisfactory patterns be identified which will lead to successful work with the patient?

These and related questions were in the mind of the researcher as he dealt with this particular aspect of the clinical problem.

THE PLACE OF THE COMMUNITY CLINIC

The current trend is to think in terms of community clinics

---

[23] For a more complete discussion of the similarities and differences see Ruth B. Freeman: *Public Health Nursing Practice,* Philadelphia, W. B. Saunders Co., 1957, p. 49.

giving a variety of services to the parents and thus enabling the mother to keep the child at home and not only to cope with him but to improve considerably his functioning ability. This concept of the community clinic was accepted as the basic focus for the present study. This leads to the question: What are the programs that parents value, and what programs do clinics see as being most important for the home? We shall therefore examine as wide a variety of services as possible to evaluate their relevance for both the mother (or the parents) and the clinic. We will also try to determine whether parents to any considerable degree seem to be interested in institutionalization for their retarded child and what kinds of behavior problems are most apt to bring on this parental desire. The desire to institutionalize the child is to be regarded as opposite of the prevailing pattern whereby about 96 per cent of the retarded are living in the community. However, it still is necessary for a community clinic to know at what point placement in an institutional setting is desirable or necessary either for the health of the patient, the mother, or other members of the family. It was, therefore, with this aspect in mind that the research plan included a look at the parents who said they wanted to place their child in a training school.

Chapter II

METHOD OF STUDY

T HE METHODOLOGY OF the study is presented herewith in outline form: (a) The study was conceived as being exploratory in nature; (b) no hypotheses were therefore formulated; (c) a "data-guide" was employed which helped structure the interviews but did not restrain the respondent from talking in depth about any question; (d) no statistical analyses were made but instead impressions gained from a close and critical evaluation of the data were noted; (c) the case records were examined as checks on the reliability of the personal interview data; (f) staff consensus was studied through talking with various members of the staff; (g) other documents of the Cambridge Service for Retarded Children (annual reports, case conference records, etc.) were looked over, and (h) the writer personally interviewed each of the twenty-four mothers in the selected sample.

After settling on the research problem and surveying the literature, the researcher took the following steps: (a) He selected the Cambridge, Massachusetts, area for the study and specifically the Cambridge Service for Retarded Children; (b) he compiled demographic data related to population (including school population and general characteristics); (c) he set up a research design; (d) he conducted interviews with the mothers in their homes; (e) he made an analysis of the interview data, the case records, related documents, and interviews with the staff; (f) he added six cases not in the CSRC as a "contrast" group, and (g) he wrote a report of the study and had data and findings examined by the staff of the CSRC.

The Sample

The sample was chosen on a "time cohort" basis, starting with July, 1958. This would allow sufficient time to have elapsed since the opening of the agency. The criteria for selection were: The child (a) must have been classified as "brain damaged"; (b) must have an IQ of approximately 54 or less, and (c) must have a chronological age of not more than ten years. The cases were selected as they were listed in the case records, if they fitted the above criteria. Twenty-four such cases were found out of an active case load of 115 children.[1]

It will be noted that the IQ score of 54 or less encompasses three categories of retardation according to the revised terminology.[2] The sample, however, did not contain any "profoundly" retarded children.

The Study Design

The study was planned as an inquiry into how a specific group of mothers perceived their retarded child, and what were their actions in seeking and utilizing services. The best method seemed to be a field study approach with a focused interview. The advantages of this method were related to the fact that a formal schedule of questions might well be an inhibiting factor, while a focused interview using a "data guide" could be flexible enough to allow the interviewer to start from any one of four or five major points.

Once this decision was made, a data guide was constructed

---

[1] Cambridge Service For Retarded Children, *Annual Report to the Children's Bureau,* for the period July 1, 1959–June 30, 1960, for the case load as of June 30, 1960.

[2] Rick Heber: "Modifications in the manual on terminology and classification in mental retardation. *Amer J Ment Defic,* No. 4, 65:499-500, January, 1961.

Word Description of Retardation in Measured Intelligence	Corresponding Range in IQ Score (SD = 15)
Borderline	70-84
Mild	55-69
Moderate	40-54
Severe	25-39
Profound	Less than 25

around the five research questions. Other questions were sub-
headed under each of the five main questions. In addition,
detailed information (not necessarily asked of the respondent)
was secured in regard to the family characteristics: passiveness
or aggressiveness regarding services; housing conditions; number
and sex of siblings; general health of members of the family;
educational level; socioeconomic status, and other related questions. (See the complete Data Guide in the Appendix.)

This guide was pretested on five mothers who were not
included in the sample. Two changes resulted from the pretest:
(a) A decision was made to interview only mothers and not both
parents at the same time. This decision was made after several
attempts at interviewing both parents proved confusing and not
productive of completed, accurate information, and (b) questions
which would develop information regarding socioeconomic status,
education, and recreational patterns were added to the original
guide. The data guide in its amended form was then used in all
twenty-four cases in the sample. No further changes were found
necessary.

The Interviews

All interviews were conducted in the home of the respondent
with one exception. Telephone appointments were made after
the mothers indicated their willingness in response to a letter of
introduction from the CSRC which asked for their cooperation.
The one exception noted above was of a mother who never
allowed anyone in her home. The CSRC social worker and public
health nurse had also been refused admittance. The mother was
quite willing, however, to come to the CSRS office and spent
about two hours there in the interview.

Although the interviewer did not feel that the respondents
were holding back information, it was necessary on occasion to
probe further to get the mother's perceptions at the time of the
original crisis situation. A similar problem appears in almost
every study separated in time from the actual date of occurrence.
Gerhart Saenger[3] talks of the "co-mingling" of "subjective" and

---

[3] Gerhart Saenger, *Factors Influencing the Institutionalization of Mentally
Retarded Individuals in New York City.* A report to the New York State Interdepartmental Health Resources Board, January, 1960, p. 20.

"objective" pictures of the retarded as a result of this time lapse. He comments, "While it may appear at first glance that this may be a decided handicap, one must recognize that the reality of the retarded person's adjustment is inseparable from the way the family perceives the retarded child."[4] This same reasoning was applied to the present study, even though an attempt was made to get back to the crisis situation. Sometimes a further probe proved most enlightening, although frequently it was best to do this later in the conversation so as not to call attention to the fact that the respondent was being "tested."

The Case Records

Records were examined to obtain birth dates of the family, income, number of children, education, and other basic data. They were used also to verify what the respondent has said about "paths to seeking services," and what was actual record of agencies used prior to the CSRC, if any. Lastly, they gave data on the actual services considered by the staff but not offered or rendered.

Analysis of Data

After the interviews and the examination of the case records, the data were analyzed and the findings tabulated under the following rubrics:

(A) The kinds of behavior or condition that led to the suspicion of mental retardation.

(1) A separate breakdown was prepared of the same question but related only to Mongolism. Which mothers *were* told at birth of child that it was Mongoloid and which mothers were *not* told. The number of months before the child was brought to a service correlated with class status and education.

(B) Types of persons that influenced the mother to bring the patient to the CSRC or other service.

(C) The services wanted by the parents, offered and rendered by the CSRC, rejected or not offered nor available.

[4] *Ibid.*

(D) Services the mothers reported as "helping' to alleviate or modify their problems. This was broken down into "help to the child" and "help to the parents," medical or physical service and nonmedical or nonphysical.

(E) Socioeconomic status was related to various factors, such as coping ability, acceptance, institutionalization, parents "talking over" problems, parent relationships, satisfactions regarding services, services that alleviate problems, and types of persons having influence.

(F) The variable of religion was related to the same factors as listed above in rubric E. The differences in relation to the above factors, however, were not significant enough to warrant completion, due to the small size of the sample.

(G) Paths to consultation and action.

Staff Consensus

A part of the analysis that was left unstructured dealt with interviewing various staff members regarding consensus. The object here was to ascertain (a) the customary degree of consensus regarding treatment—a point which was directly related to how the staff regarded the client; (b) what the usual disagreements were about; (c) how the staff functioned as a team in giving service; (d) whether agreement was by mutual consent or after a certain amount of "forced" or "pseudo" consensus, and (e) whether the staff came to consensus even though one or more members had a strong emotional involvement in carrying a case personally. The answers to these questions could not be readily achieved through a printed schedule but rather were developed through a series of informal, unstructured meetings with each member of the staff over a period of about ten months.

Contrast Cases

After the study was in progress it was decided to attempt to locate a sample of families who had children which fitted the criteria of the study, but who, for one reason or another, had not gone to the CSRC. It was felt that this contrast group might provide clues as to the number and type of families that go elsewhere for services. Six such families were located who had gone to the Walter E. Fernald State School at Waverley, Massachusetts. The results are presented in Chapter IV.

Social Stratification

This study had as one of its important considerations the place of the social class variable in the patterns of help-seeking, of perceptions, and of value placing on services rendered. It was necessary, therefore, to find a way of stratifying the sample which would not be too complicated or elaborate considering the sample size.

An informal system was used with four criteria: (a) the location and condition of the home; (b) the education of the father; (c) the occupation of the father, and (d) family income.[5] The sample was stratified by the writer and verified separately with two staff members of the CSRC. It was not found necessary to utilize a scale such as Warner's "Index of Status Characteristics" or Hollingshead's "Index of Social Position" in order to stratify the sample into social class terminology. The terms lower-lower, upper-lower, lower-middle, and upper-middle were understood consistently enough by the three persons ranking the sample as to give little difficulty. By agreement, and after discussion with the study director of the CSRC (Simon Olshansky), the consensus was that there were no upper-class persons either in the whole clinic program or in the sample. This limited the ranking to the four classes mentioned above. Of course any subjective type ranking is subject to error and real questions arise as to what is lower-middle-class, for example, rather than upper-lower.[6] The Warner terminology, however, seemed to offer

---

[5] W. Lloyd Warner uses four criteria: occupation, source of income, house type, and dwelling area. These categories are weighted and multiplied by a score assigned to each characteristic within the category to obtain an I.S.C. The Hollingshead "Index of Social Position" uses residence, occupation, and education, and by a similar method arrives at an I.S.P. score. Both these methods were not considered appropriate for the type and size of sample of this study.

[6] If we are to arrive at any scientific analysis of society, some sort of definition is a necessary tool. C. Wright Mills, questioning whether the white collar workers are a 'new middle class', or a 'new working class,' says that the solution, while not solely resting upon definition, ". . . its empirical solution is made possible only by clarified definitions." See C. Wright Mills: *White Collar*. New York, Oxford University Press, 1956, p. 295.

enough room for agreement on what is "usually" meant by the various classifications. Interestingly enough, the rank assignments made by the writer were almost identical with those by the other two persons involved. The differences of opinion followed the pattern mentioned by Hollingshead and Redlich in their New Haven study[7] in that they were never more than one class position away from each other. These differences were resolved by a vote of all three persons.

The use of the terms "blue collar" and "white collar" workers was considered as a possible means of classification but was discarded in favor of the Warner terminology. The description of life-style and work-style of these two groups was found to be a useful concept, however, in roughing out the main outlines of the sample.

The term "blue collar" workers is usually used to refer to those persons who are manual workers, usually on a weekly wage, with wives who usually stay at home and have no career aspirations, and who themselves rarely have completed high school. The term "white collar" workers is usually used to describe a middle-class group of persons who may be clerks, sales people, teachers, officials, or businessmen; whose salaries most frequently are on a per annum basis or commissions; whose wives very frequently are employed, and who, educationally, have finished high school and may have gone to college. Financially, this latter group is usually a little better off than the former, although with the higher pay in some skilled trades there is some merging of salary scales at the lower end.[8]

If we use only the terms "blue collar" and "white collar,"

---

[7] Hollingshead and Redlich, *op. cit.*, p. 389.

[8] For some recent references regarding social class terminology and the use of these terms as descriptive of positions occupied in the social hierarchy, see Lee Rainwater, Richard P. Coleman, and Gerald Handel: *Workingman's Wife: Her Personality, World and Life Style.* New York, Oceana Publications, Inc., 1959; W. Lloyd Warner, Marchia Meeker, and Kenneth Eells: *Social Class in America.* New York, Harper Torchbooks, 1960; Kurt B. Mayer: *Class and Society.* New York, Random House, Re Ed, 1955; Hollingshead and Redlich, *op. cit.*, pp. 66-136; Lee Rainwater: *And the Poor Get Children.* Chicago, Quadrangle Books, 1960; Walter B. Miller: Implications of urban lower-class culture for social work. *The Social Service Review*, No. 3, Vol. 33, September, 1959.

we obviously lose the niceties of gradation which actually exist. Within the blue collar group there is hierarchy from the lowest broom pusher to the expert technician working with his hands. Likewise, there is a vast difference between the president or vice-president of a company and the five-and-dime clerks, although both are correctly identified as white collar workers.

The decision to use the Warner terminology is based on its utility in making possible an understanding of the different gradations within the class structure. It should not be necessary to point out that no invidious comparisons or moral or value judgments are intended or implied in the use of the terms "lower-lower-class," or "lower-middle-class."

Limitations of this Study

Certain problems were recognized as being inherent in a study of this kind. First, the sample is small and drawn entirely from one agency where the clients had sought help. The element of "self selection" therefore is a variable that may alter the patterns in some systematic way unknown to the investigator. Second, the patterns uncovered may not be unique to mothers with retarded children, but may also include those whose children have other handicaps or no handicaps at all. Third, the study must draw upon the memory of the mothers in obtaining the retrospective data. Fourth, the sample, although representative of the high percentage of Roman Catholics in the agency and of the community may vary because of that fact in some consistent way not necessarily true, let us say, of a heavily Protestant community.

These limitations, however, are not believed to invalidate any of the findings for the following reasons: (a) No attempt has been made to generalize the specific findings of this study; (b) the findings are related only to the mothers of a specific sub-sample; children under ten years of age, diagnosed as brain damaged, and with an IQ of under 54; (c) no hypotheses were formulated and tested although some assumptions were examined; (d) the retrospective data indicate what mothers *think* is true. (this is as important as any other "fact" and just as much of a reality to the mother), and (e) attention has been called to the high percentage of Roman Catholics in the sample. The reader is thus forewarned not to generalize from this sample as to other cases where the population may be similarly skewed in the direction of Protestant or other faiths.

The writer was encouraged to undertake the research involved in the face of these limitations by a statement made by Howard R. Kelman: "If research awaited the resolution of all of the difficult problems that are faced, nothing would ever be done."[9]

---

[9] In personal correspondence to the writer.

Chapter III

THE CHILDREN, THE FAMILIES, AND THE
SERVICE PROGRAM

The TWENTY-FOUR families in the sample had a total of eighty-eight children. Only two of the families were broken, in both cases through separation. The ages of the retarded children range from two years to 9.7, for an average of 5.7 years.

Since this community had a very high percentage of Roman Catholic families, it is not surprising that of the sample 79 per cent of the families were Catholic, and 21 per cent Protestant. There were no Jewish families.

THE CHILDREN

There seemed not to be any pattern in the ordinal position of the retarded children in the families. In the largest group in the sample (three-child family), five were the first born, of whom two were Mongoloid; four were second children, of whom one was Mongoloid, and five were third children, with one Mongoloid. In these fourteen three-child families, there were four Mongoloids; in the two four-child families there was one, and also one in the three five-child families. In the one six-child family there was no Mongoloid, and in the two seven-child families, one. It can be seen, therefore, that the distribution of Mongoloids was unrelated to the size of the family. In all twenty-four cases, for example, the first child was retarded in seven, the second in five, the third in six, the fourth in three, the fifth in two, and the seventh in one. (See Table I.)

Speech Problems of the Retarded. According to the parents

their most difficult problem with their retarded child was in relation to his lack of speech, or its unintelligibility. Instinctively perhaps the parents felt that if only the child could or would talk that somehow they could get through to him. In order to examine the elements of this problem in more detail it was decided to classify the speech problems of the children according to the following Schonnel and Watts[1] criteria:

A. Normal.

B. Below Normal: Intelligible but with certain indistinctness of articulation or pronunciation.

C. Very much below normal: Extremely difficult to follow; intelligible usually only to parents.

D. Completely unintelligible or lacking in speech.

Of the sample of twenty-four children, only one could be classified as having normal speech; nine were below normal, of whom four were Mongoloid. Three children were very much below normal. In the lowest group, that classified as completely unintelligible or with no speech, there were eleven, of whom three were Mongoloid. It can be seen from this classification that even in the case of Mongoloid children speech may vary from what is quite intelligible to none at all. It needs to be stressed here, however, that this is only in reference to speech

TABLE I
ORDINAL POSITION

No. of Families	Size of Family	Ordinal Position of Retarded Child
1	One-child family	
1	Two-child family	Second child (only one case)
14	Three-child family	5 were first child (2 Mongoloid)
		4 were second child (1 Mongoloid)
		5 were third child (1 Mongoloid)
2	Four-child family	1 was fourth (Mongoloid)
		1 was first child
3	Five-child family	2 were fifth child (1 Mongoloid)
		1 was fourth child
1	Six-child family	1 was third child
2	Seven-child family	1 was seventh child (Mongoloid)
—		1 was fourth child
24		

[1] F. J. Schonnel, and B. H. Watts: A first survey of the effects of a subnormal child in the family unit. *Amer J Ment Defic*, No. 1, *61*:210-219, July 1956.

and does not consider language skills. In the latter case, it would be probably true that all these children would fall very much below normal. See Table II on speech.

TABLE II
SPEECH, DIAGNOSIS, AND STIGMATA

Case	Normal	Below Normal	Very Much Below Normal	No Speech	Diagnosis	STIGMATA Yes	No
1	—	(M)	—	—	Mongoloid	x	—
2	—	—	—	x	Brain damage-unspecified	—	x
3	—	—	—	x	Cerebral palsy with mental deficiency	x	—
4	—	—	—	(M)	Mongoloid	x	—
5	—	(M)	—	—	Mongoloid	x	—
6	—	—	—	x	Mongoloid	x	—
7	—	—	—	x	Spastic paraplegic-brain damage	x	—
8	—	(M)	—	—	Mongoloid	x	—
9	—	—	—	x	Microcephalic	—	x
10	—	—	—	x	Questionable etiology	—	x
11	—	x	—	—	Neurological damage, question of Epilepsy	—	x
12	—	—	—	x	Organic impairment, questionable etiology	—	x
13	—	—	x	—	Early development defect, questionable etiology	—	x
14	—	(M)	—	—	Mongoloid	x	—
15	—	x	—	—	Brain damage	—	x
16	—	—	—	(M)	Mongoloid	x	—
17	—	x	—	—	Mild cerebral spastic diplegia	—	x
18	—	x	—	—	Severe emotional disturbance	—	x
19	—	—	x	—	Turner's syndrome, congenital heart defect	x	—
20	—	—	x	—	Cretin	—	x
21	x	—	—	—	Questionable etiology, MR, emotional	—	x
22	—	—	—	(M)	Mongoloid	x	—
23	—	—	—	x	Demyelinating disease	x	—
24	—	x	—	—	Cerebral deficit	—	x
Total	1	9	3	11		12	12

The type of behavior in these children that first aroused the mother's suspicion that there was something abnormal was the child's failure to sit or crawl at the proper age, slowness to develop, poor coordination or lack of it, and slowness in talking.

The children in this sample were brought to the medical attention of either a clinic or a doctor at an early age, as Table III shows.

One might assume that, in general, the parents would bring

TABLE III
AGE OF ARRIVAL AT CLINIC OR DOCTOR

No. of Cases	Class	Average Months
1	Upper-middle-class	36 months (only 1 case)
11	Lower-middle-class	22.1 months
7	Upper-lower-class	24.6 months
5	Lower-lower-class	12.2 months

their children to a doctor or clinic *earlier* if the children were obviously retarded or marked in some way with one or more stigmata. However, in the twenty-four cases, twelve could be classified as having some stigmata which seemed more or less obvious (see Table II) and which might indicate some condition, possibly retardation, while the other twelve had no stigmata at all. Of the whole group of retarded children, seven were classified as Mongoloid and therefore also as having stigmata. The presence of such visual evidence of abnormality did not seem to be a factor in the parents bringing the children for treatment; behavior seemed instead to be the motivating force.

THE FAMILIES

The families came from an economic group with annual incomes ranging from $2,511 to $6,760. The median figure was $4,180. An average family in the sample could be described as having been married 11.6 years, having a take home pay of eighty dollars a week, and having three children who were in the second, third, and fifth grades. The children generally were getting good or acceptable grades and, with two exceptions, were not retarded in any way. As previously mentioned, 79 per cent were Roman Catholic, due in part to the fact that this area in Cambridge is very highly populated by Catholic families. In regard to education, most of the parents had had approximately the same education, usually at least high school or some high school for both parents. Twenty-three of them had had at least some high school; only thirteen reported themselves as having had not more than eighth grade; nine reported some schooling after high school, and in most cases this was business school for the mother; and three parents (two fathers and one mother) had had a college education. The typical family lived in a rented apartment in a poor area of Cambridge, for which it paid about sixty-five dollars. The apartment, however, was well kept, clean, and adequate in respect to heating but inadequate as to the number of rooms. The father was a manual worker about forty-two years old; the mother a housewife approximately thirty-six years of age. She had little or no interests outside of the home. In fact, she rarely left the home, perhaps not for weeks on end. For recreation, she and her husband looked at television in the evenings and on rare occasions went out together to see a movie. Usually, however, the man or the woman went alone because of the difficulty of getting a baby-sitter and paying her. Occasionally they visited relatives or friends or had them come in for an evening of card playing or talking.

The usual complaint was "inadequate income." These families had to be extremely careful in their purchases, and their first interest was to provide food and a roof over their heads. The matter of food played an important part in the lower-class working family and in the lower-middle-class group. The typical family said that it ate well because, "If you can't eat, what else do you have?" The family lived in crowded conditions. Even though the average number of children in the sample was only 3.7 per family, the rooms were usually too small and too crowded. The mother felt that the small apartment with inadequate ventilation and inadequate space for the children to run and play created a difficult situation for her. She was usually harassed and found herself exhausted at the end of the day from her constant yelling and running around after the children. Her admonitions all day long: "Be quiet," "Go and play," "Look at television," or "No more cookies now," and so forth, seemed a constant repetition of "don'ts" and demands that the children seemed to slough off after a while and hardly notice. All of her exertions and the constant pressure of children underfoot, especially when complicated with a mentally retarded child, left the mother very tired. In the group under study, however, the mothers' health, except for the complaint of tiredness, seemed to be surprisingly good. In only a couple of cases was "nervousness" mentioned as a symptom by the mother. One mother who reported herself in good health was found afterwards, upon the probing of the interviewer, to remember that she "had gallstones!" The lack of complaint about physical ailments seems to correlate with a relatively high coping ability in the group. Bernard Farber has pointed to evidence that the mothers in low status groups tend to develop poor physical health in cases where there is "role organization crises."[2] In the group we have under study, the mothers, for the most part, were able to cope with their mentally retarded children and so we may assume that they did not confront a role organization crisis, nor consequently display symptomatic "physical illness."

Size of Families　The twenty-four families had a total of eighty-eight children or 3.7 per family. Over half of the families (63 per cent) had an average of three children. (See Table IV which indicates that the three-child family occured in fourteen out of the twenty-four cases.

Occupation of the Father. Of the twenty-four fathers, two were classified as professionals (one research physicist and one substitute teacher); four as clerks and kindred workers; seventeen as manual workers, and one as a service worker.

TABLE IV
SIZE OF FAMILIES

Number of Children in Family	Number of Families
1	1
2	1
3	14
4	2
5	3
6	1
7	2
	24 Total

Using the Warner Revised Scale, these were rated for their occupation and found to have good correlation with the class level assigned.[3] (See Tables V and VI.) It can be seen from these tables that the majority of the fathers fall into the fourth, fifth and sixth ratings of the Warner scale and the totals for these groups are nineteen out of the twenty-four.[4]

---

[2] Bernard Farber, Perceptions of crisis and related variables in the impact of a retarded child on the mother. *J. Health Hum Behav*, No. 2, *1*:108-118, Summer, 1960.

[3] The occupation of the father, according to Johnson, mainly determines class rank; see Harry M. Johnson: *Sociology: A Systematic Introduction.* New York, Harcourt, Brace and Co., 1960, p. 470.

[4] For a description of this scale see W. Lloyd Warner, Marchia Meeker, and

Occupation of the Mother. Twenty-three of the mothers classified themselves as housewives. Of this group, only three engaged in some sort of part time work in addition to their housework. One mother did home sewing and helped with odd jobs; one worked for two or three hours a week doing a little bookkeeping for a corner store, and the third did some typing at home which did not interfere greatly with her caring for the home. The one working mother, who was separated from her husband, received something from him every month for the care of the retarded child and for her other child by their marriage, and worked as a waitress in a local restaurant. It is interesting to note that the mothers seemed to feel that their place was in the home and that they had a really important job to do there. Even in the case of mothers who were trained to go out and earn, either because of business school training or, as in one case, through a college education, there was no attempt to do so. With one or two rare exceptions, in which cases the mothers attempted to help the family income by taking jobs on occasion, they seemed satisfied with their position in the home and the responsibilities that they had there.

THE SERVICE PROGRAM

The services of CSRC are planned for the entire family. This has been a policy of the Cambridge Service for Retarded Children since its opening in the fall of 1957. An article in the American Journal of Public Health by Edward Wellin recommends this policy:

> Categorically one could say that services for the retarded child cannot effectively be rendered or any realistic plans be made for him without considering the health and other problems of the total family unit. Hence, it is really necessary to deal with a retarded child as the index case or entree into the family situation.[5]

The program of service, therefore, is divided into care for the child and for the family as a whole. The staff consists of eight workers: the medical doctor who serves as clinical director,

Kenneth Eells: *Social Class in America* New York, Harper Torch Book, 1960, p. 165.

    [5] Edward Wellin *et al., op. cit.,* p. 42.

TABLE V

STRATIFICATION AND RATINGS ON OCCUPATION[6]

[6] Based on Warner's "Revised Scale for Rating Occupation." See *Ibid.*, pp. 140-141.

Social Class	*1*	*2*	*3*	*4*	*5*	*6*	*7*	*Totals*
Upper-middle	1							1
Lower-middle			2	5	4			11
Upper-lower				2	2	3		7
Lower-lower					1	2	2	5
Totals	1	0	2	7	7	5	2	24

TABLE VI

OCCUPATION OF THE FATHER

Rating Assigned to Occupation (*Based on W. Lloyd Warner scale*)	*Professional*	*Clerks and Kindred Workers, etc.*	*Manual Workers*	*Protective and Service Workers*
1	Research Physicist (20)			
2				
3	Teacher, substitute (15)	Postal clerk (11)		
4		Lab Technician (7) Scheduler (13) Office work (19)	Printer (6) Supt. Warehouse (9) Tool maker (16) Truck dispatcher (24)	
5			Welder (2) Lineman (4) Blade inspector (8) TV repair (14) Iron worker (18) Plumber (21)	Driver-salesman (10)
6			Jewel polisher (1) Mill operator (3) Mixer (5) Auto painter (12) Candy maker (17)	
7			Laborer (22) Grinder (23)	
Totals	2	4	17	1

Note: There were no proprietors, managers, businessmen, farmers in the sample. (Case Numbers in parentheses.)

a study director, a public health nurse, a psychiatric social worker, a psychologist, a nutritionist, a nursery school teacher, and a secretary. The medical director, psychologist, and nutritionist provide part-time services; the remainder of the staff are employed full time. The staff provides not only diagnostic but also treatment services through speech therapy, the nursery school, and other physical help such as the home training program or the public health nurse. In addition, when appropriate or necessary, the staff makes referrals to other social agencies who render treatment or other services as needed.

Chapter IV

THE MOTHERS

THE INTERVIEWS WERE conducted almost exclusively with the mothers. In several cases the fathers were also present and in one case where the mother was away the father was interviewed instead. The interviewer used the data-guide but made every attempt to have the mother feel at ease by not questioning her item by item. The interviewer, therefore, usually began by asking the mother to tell about the present behavior of the child and what she saw as the current problems. The answers given by the mother were then related to the five major categories of analysis: (a) What in the child's behavior caused the mother to suspect mental retardation? (b) What types of persons had conspicuous influence on the mother's bringing (or not bringing) the child to an agency giving services to the mentally retarded? (c) What services were offered and rendered by a specialized community agency for mentally retarded children and their families? (d) What services were used by the mothers? (e) What services did mothers report as alleviating or modifying the problems they faced by having a mentally retarded child in the family?

KINDS OF BEHAVIOR LEADING TO SUSPICION OF MENTAL RETARDATION

The data seem to show that the mothers are not aware early of mental retardation as a possibility. The mothers consistently think of their children as having some physical ailment. For example, of all the behavioral conditions reported the one that was of concern to most mothers was "not sitting up properly and crawling at the ages expected." The next item in number of cases mentioned was "slowness of development"; the third, "poor coordination and lack of muscle control"; the fourth, "slow talking" and (sometimes mentioned with this) "blurred speech." The item most often commented upon by relatives, friends and neighbors was the first one mentioned above, that of not sitting or crawling at the proper time. These replies, however, are not to be construed as meaning that the mothers thought that the children were mentally retarded because of this slowness. Almost invariably they can be quoted as saying that they went to the clinic or the doctor about this suspicious behavior because they thought there was something wrong physically. It might take months or even years before the mothers came to attribute this slowness to mental retardation. Only after some difficult sessions with the doctor did the mothers come to see that the problem was one of retardation. Frequently, when the mother reported the doctor's diagnosis to the father, he reacted violently, claiming that his child was not retarded and that the mother should spend more time training him, helping his speech, helping him to sit up, or taking the child out in a stroller; in other words, the father thought that the mother could train the child if only she would. In the twenty-four cases studied, most indications are that the mother did not suspect mental retardation in all of the four items mentioned above. Even in those cases where the mother did indicate she was "suspicious" (of mental retardation), the writer wondered if this was not hindsight rather than the thinking of the mother at the time she took her child to the doctor.

The fact is that mothers often do not recognize their children as possibly retarded mentally even when to professional eyes they are "obvious cases," such as Mongolism. In the sample studied there were seven Mongoloids. Of the seven mothers, five had *not* been told of the condition at birth. In almost every case, the features of the child did not indicate Mongolism either to the mother or the father, and in most cases the parents saw the child as perfectly normal and in no way different from their other children, although in some cases they did mention that the child was slow. Of the five cases mentioned, one mother took her child at the age of six months to the doctor, questioning why its tongue protruded all the time, but this same mother emphasized to the interviewer that she did not see the patient as being different from her other children. Perhaps this is borne out by the fact that, although this mother took the child at the age of six months to the doctor for the specific question mentioned, she did not go to the CSRC until the child was sixty-one months old. This mother, for example, had a great deal of difficulty in adjusting to the fact that her child was Mongoloid and retarded. She reported "that she was terribly upset" and did not know quite what to do and was very concerned that the child was retarded and yet she did not really understand what Mongolism meant. The father, on the other hand, told the mother that it meant that the child was "insane" and would have to be placed in a mental hospital as quickly as possible. It was then necessary for the doctor to explain to both parents that Mongoloid children may be kept at home for quite a while. He did not specify how long and this particular child was kept in the home until he was almost nine years of age. The mother said, "God sent him to me, so I'll keep him." This mother had a number of normal children and yet could not bring herself to see the patient as being really abnormal. When at the age of five she took him to the CSRC it was with the intention of placing him in the nursery school, but since he was not toilet-trained the school could not accept him. The public health nurse, too, over a long period of time attempted to train the patient, but even with this extra help the mother was unable to get the patient to comply, or to work out any effective training schedule. When the patient was finally sent to a state school at almost nine years of age, he was still not toilet-trained. This mother was of the lower-lower-class with a tenth or eleventh grade education.

In another case, a Mrs. B., who also had a Mongoloid child, did not see anything wrong with the child for almost four and one half months. At that time she took the child to the clinic for a checkup and the doctor asked her who the child looked like. The mother was suspicious because the doctor repeated this question a number of times, but apparently was unable to answer him, and he finally said to the mother, "This boy looks like a Mongoloid baby." The mother did not know what that meant but was afraid it was something bad. She did not raise any questions, however, with the doctor but instead, as she puts it, "bundled up the child and took him home." The mother repeated to the interviewer that she didn't see anything wrong with the child at that time. He looked "pretty normal to me," she said, "sure he is slower than the other children, but he was my first, and I didn't have anything to go by." This mother is upper-lower-class with an eleventh grade education. She waited fifty-six months before taking the child to the CSRC.

Of the two mothers that were told at the birth of their children that they were Mongoloid, one was terribly shocked. She reported that when she first heard it she refused to think about it, and although she was told that there was a clinic that could help her, she did not want to take the child there and instead waited for three months. She did bring the child at that time and has been a client of the service ever since. This early use of professional service might be the reason the child was functioning at a high level considering the degree of retardation (a below fifty IQ). This mother is upper-lower-class with a sixth grade education. The other mother who was told at birth that her child was Mongoloid did not understand Mongolism or that it meant mental retardation. This mother went along for a period of sixty-one months before taking her child to the CSRC. Perhaps in this case the mother, since she did not understand what Mongolism meant, was further confused by the doctor to whom she went for the child's physical examination after a period of six or seven weeks. This doctor reassured her that the patient would probably be "all right. Give him a couple of years and we will see what will develop." This is an unfortunate kind of reassurance that apparently has been given in a number of other cases. The mother, and sometimes the father, then believes that the child is really normal, but has some peculiar facial feature, or has something wrong with the tongue and therefore cannot speak, or is slow for some other physical reason. Thus, the patient is deprived of professional care. In the opinion of Dorothy Durling and Clemens E. Benda, this is especially unfortunate in the case of Mongoloids. They point out that proper and early treatment of Mongoloid children can improve their physical appearance and also help them maintain a higher IQ than is usually found in untreated cases.[1]

In the case cited above, the mother whom we shall call "Mrs. N," an upper-lower-class mother with an eighth grade education, did not understand that her child was mentally retarded nor see the child's Mongolism as a sign of retardation. The mother, although pressured by friends and relatives, waited until the child was sixty-one months of age before taking him to the CSRC. It should be noted that this was true even though the mother *had been told at birth* that the child was Mongoloid. Contrary to the common assumption in this matter, parents do not necessarily know what is meant by "Mongolism" and when used by professionals the term, unless thoroughly explained, may have no meaning at all and may not be related to retardation in the mind of the parent. As has been indicated, taking the child to a clinic for professional service as early as possible may very well result in helping the child to function on his highest possible level. Waiting for years may mean that the child will function at a much lower and perhaps a discouraging level, as far as the parents are concerned, so that institutionalization at an earlier age than necessary may be considered by them.

TYPES OF PERSONS HAVING CONSPICUOUS INFLUENCE ON THE PARENTS BRINGING (OR NOT BRINGING) THE CHILD TO AN AGENCY

In order to examine the responses to this question, the pattern was broken down into two sections. One had to do with the "first steps" taken by the parents to get some kind of help and the second was related to the types of persons who actually influenced the parents to go to the CSRC. In regard to the first part, the parents in fifteen out of twenty-four cases went directly to the medical doctor; in five cases they discussed the child with a nurse prior to making a decision, and in four cases finally made

---

[1] Dorothy Durling and Clemens E. Benda: Mental growth curves in untreated institutionalized Mongoloid patients. *Amer J Men Defic*, No. 3, 56:578, January, 1952.

the decision on their own to go to a doctor or to a clinic because they had some questions about the normalcy of their child, although they might have talked either to a doctor or a nurse or both. In these cases of "self-referral," the mother almost invariably had talked with a medical person, either a doctor, a nurse in a clinic, or with a private physician, so that she was already suspicious about the child's abnormality.

By the time the mother was finally ready to go to the CSRC, she had undoubtedly made up her mind that the child was retarded. This can be partly substantiated by the fact that fewer doctors seemed to be involved in the final decision to come to CSRC. The assumption here is that doctors are more likely to be involved in early diagnosis. Then the mother comes to realize from the diagnosis given, and sometimes from shopping around to confirm this diagnosis, that the child is in fact retarded. The mother then goes through a long torturous period during which she must decide whether or not to take the child for some type of treatment. Usually the mother has no definite idea of what kind of treatment or service is available or might help, but finally after this long period of waiting she does decide to take the child and so makes a move that may become recorded as a "self-referral." The case records of the CSRC show a number of such self-referrals which on closer analysis reveals almost without question prior visits by the mother to many professional people. The Children's Medical Center in Boston has been instrumental, for example, in influencing mothers to go to the CSRC, but a number of mothers report going on their own (which is then recorded as a self-referral), even after talking with another doctor or a nurse.

The actual count of types of persons responsible for influencing the mothers to go to the CSRC was as follows: nine referrals by the Children's Medical Center (these were all counted as referrals from doctors); seven by nurses (including public health nurses); five self-referrals; two by the Cambridge Guidance Clinic, and one by the Boston Association for Retarded Children.

The three typical patterns for referral to the CSRC seem to be (a) contact with a nurse, either one in the hospital or a public health nurse; (b) self-referrals, and (c) contact with clinics and medical staff. A few illustrations will show these patterns.

Mrs. B. This mother brought her child into the hospital for a hernia operation at the age of three and one half years. The attending nurse became very friendly with the mother and explained that she too had a retarded child, that this was nothing to be ashamed of, and recommended that the mother go to the CSRC. The mother at first did nothing about this and, in fact, was quite surprised at the statement that the child was retarded. Although the child is Mongoloid, the mother did not recognize him as being in any way different or retarded. Some time later a public health nurse received a call from the hospital nurse about the condition and followed through by phoning the mother and asking whether she would like to come in to the CSRC. It is interesting to note that even with this aggressive action on the part of the public health nurse it was still necessary to contact the mother four or five times before she conceded that the child needed diagnosis and possible treatment. Here we see a case where the mother has been told that the child was Mongoloid when he was only four and one-half months old, but, not believing the statement, she continued to take the child to clinics other than the CSRC until he was fifty-six months old. Even then it took four or five contacts to get the mother to take the child to the CSRC.

Mrs. G. This mother responded very quickly to the recommendation of the visiting nurse who discovered the child in question, later diagnosed as a spastic paraplegic. At that time the patient was nineteen months of age. The mother had been only twenty years old when she gave birth to the patient, her fourth child. The mother was very young and quite worn and exhausted from raising the family, since she had married right after the tenth grade and began to have a family immediately. She seemed in a very receptive frame of mind to the nurse's suggestion that the patient be taken to the CSRC.

Mrs. X. This mother had gone to a doctor from the time of the child's birth and realized that there was something abnormal but related this to some physical problem, feeling that speech was the greatest difficulty. The mother had gone to the Children's Medical Center, as well as to the Boston University Speech Clinic, in order to obtain help for her child. She had enrolled him in a public school, but when he was unable to perform as he should the mother received a visit from a public health nurse who explained the problem in detail. This mother then, in response to the positive act of the public health nurse, did take the child to the CSRC.

In each of these three examples the mother needed aggressive help from a nurse in order finally to decide to take her child to the Cambridge agency.

In the next cases to be considered the mothers took the children to the clinic on what, according to the record, has been called "self-referral." However, closer analysis seemed to reveal that these were not true self-referrals in the sense that in every case the mother had been talked to, usually at length, by the family physician, a nurse, or some clinic personnel other than CSRC. Some time elapsed, however, in almost every self-referral case before the mother was able to bring herself to the point of taking the child to the CSRC. A few cases will show this particular pattern.

Mrs. F. This mother is listed in the case records of CSRC as being a self-referral; she had read about the service in the newspapers. On examination of the pattern of help-seeking prior to coming to the Service, however, it was seen that the mother's sister had already intervened and recommended that the child be taken to the local state school for evaluation. This was done and there the mother was given information about the child's IQ which she said later didn't mean too much to her. "Well, they send you a letter," she said, meaning that although she was a high school graduate she did not understand the diagnosis completely. Consequently, she continued to look around and went to her own doctor and to the Children's Medical Center before finally going to the CSRC when the patient was thirty-seven months old. Although the mother finally did get to the CSRC on her own, so to speak, we see behind that action a long pattern of seeking help elsewhere and perhaps also of the grief a mother feels and her reluctance to accept the diagnosis. There was the constant pattern of first looking for reassurances that the child was normal and then the final acceptance that he did need further care and treatment.

Mr. and Mrs. O. When the patient was twenty-four months of age the parents were advised by the doctor that there was extensive brain damage and that the child would probably never be normal. He was then taken to the Children's Medical Center and given extensive examinations. Although no definitive diagnosis was given them at this time, the parents realized that there really was something wrong with the child, something that had been called retardation several times by doctors. However, the parents were not willing to accept this explanation of the condition. When the patient was forty-eight months old, the father went to the CSRC and said that he had read about it in the newspapers and wondered whether his child could be helped. Again we see here a pattern of the family having gone to various medical services prior to going to the Cambridge agency, even though the case records indicate "self-referral."

Mrs. V. In this case again we see a similar pattern, with the mother going to a number of medical services prior to the CSRC where she is listed as a self-referral. Actually, in tracing the case, we see that the medical profession had been in touch with this mother almost since the child's birth, advising her that he was a Mongoloid and mentally retarded. The mother was first told that the child was Mongoloid at the age of a month and a half when he came down with pneumonia. At the age of six months, he was taken to the Children's Medical Center and there diagnosed as Mongoloid with severe retardation and an estimated IQ of 20. At forty-eight months, the patient was taken to one of the state hospitals and institutionalized for a period of four months. However, it was not until the child was sixty-one months old that the mother finally took the child to the CSRC without any clinical or medical referral. It would be incorrect, however, to believe that this mother went without a lot of very strong urging, especially from her physician who pressed her to do something for this particular child. The mother resisted, however, and did not go to the Cambridge clinic until the condition became so difficult she was unable to cope with it any longer.

The major pattern that emerges from this examination is of the doctors and nurses as being the persons of most influence in bringing the mothers to the realization that their children needed help from a service such as the CSRC. A subpattern of so-called "self-referrals" is seen as developing subsequent to visits of clinics, private physicians, or nurses; there is no official referral from an agency and the case is listed as a self-referral.

Four cases out of the twenty-four did not exactly fit this pattern. One mother, for example, finally came to the CSRC through the Boston Association for Retarded Children; two parents came through the Cambridge Guidance Clinic, and one was referred by a nursery school teacher. These four cases were not completely different in all details, but seemed in general to be outside the main stream of the pattern indicated.

Socioeconomic Status. The status of the family was seen as an important variable affecting such factors as coping ability, acceptance, institutionalization, the parents "talking over" problems, parent relationships, satisfactions regarding services, services that alleviate problems, and types of persons having influence. Table VII reflects the mothers' responses to the factors listed.[2]

By class groupings and starting with the lower-lower-class, two mothers out of five felt they were unable to cope with their children. A third was ambivalent about her ability and had periods when she felt she couldn't continue any longer and would have to "give up" as she put it and place the child in an institution. These mothers (four out of five) were able to accept their children as being retarded although again we have three of the five thinking of placing the children in a state school. These mothers also did not "talk over" problems with their husbands.

---

[2] Regarding the class status categories (lower-lower, upper-lower, etc.) used in this study, attention is called to the fact that they are meaningful only within the context of the present study. No inferences respecting the use of the same terms in studies by other researchers are intended. The categories cannot be termed discrete in respect to their cut off points. The difference for example, between the lower end of the continuum called middle class and the upper-lower is impossible to pinpoint with any degree of accuracy. Nevertheless, it was felt that even with these disadvantages it was worth the effort to make the analysis from a social class base.

TABLE VII

MATERNAL RESPONSES AS RELATED TO SOCIOECONOMIC STATUS*

Social Class	Coping Ability		Acceptance of Child		Institutionalization		Parents "Talk Over" Problems		
	Able	Unable	Able	Unable	Interested	No	Yes	No	Unknown
U-M	0	1	0	1	1	0	1	0	0
L-M	11	0	11	0	1	10	9	0	2
U-L	6	1	6	1	1	6	6	1	0
L-L	3	2	4	1	2	3	0	2	3
TOTAL	20	4	21	3	5	19	16	3	5

Social Class	Parent Relationship			Re: Services rendered (Mother) Satisfaction		Services Alleviate Problems			Types of Persons Having Influence
	Good	Poor	Unknown	Satisfied	Dissatisfied	Yes	No	Don't Know	
U-M	0	0	1	1	0	1	0	0	MD=1
L-M	10	0	1	10	1	9	1	1	MD=11; nurse=4; friends=1; n.s. teacher=1; church=1
U-L	4	2	1	6	1	4	1	2	MD=6; relatives=1; church=1; nurse=2; neighbor=1
L-L	0	1	4	5	0	5	0	0	MD=4; nurse=2
TOTAL	14	3	7	22	2	19	2	3	(Figures do not add up; some mothers mentioned more than one)

Relations between husband and wife were reported as "poor" in one case and as "unknown" in four. All five mothers were satisfied with the services rendered and felt they helped alleviate problems. Types of persons reported as influencing the mothers were physicians and nurses. Of the five mothers all seemed to depend on medical advice and none mentioned relatives, friends, or neighbors as having influenced them to bring the child to the CSRC.

---

* These are the reported responses. Mothers may have varied in actual reality responses if it had been possible to obtain such information. A time of crisis for example may evoke other responses.

Of the seven upper-lower-class mothers, six reported being able and one unable to cope with the retardate. The acceptance of the child fell in the same pattern. Only one mother was interested in institutionalization. Six mothers were able to "talk over" problems. Marital relations were reported as good in four cases, poor in two and unknown in one. All except one mother was satisfied with services rendered; the one dissent was in relation to one service performed. Regarding services alleviating problems, four mothers felt that they did, one said no, and two "don't know." This group reported more different types of persons as having influenced them to bring the children to the CSRC. Several mothers mentioned more than one. Again the physicians were mentioned most often (six times), but relatives, the church (Sister Superior), and a neighbor were each mentioned once; nurse was mentioned twice. The pattern of the upper-lower-class mothers therefore seemed to be more stable. They were more able to cope with their children, had a better marital relationship, were able to talk with their husbands, and apparently felt it necessary to talk with more people in order to strengthen their desire to go to a clinic such as the CSRC. They relied much more on medical help than was assumed. The pattern for this and the lower-lower-class group seemed to be in favor of medical advice although the upper-lower group seemed to feel the need for the extra confirmation.

The eleven lower-middle-class mothers presented a distinct and solid pattern of reporting and being able to cope with their retardate. There was acceptance and understanding. Only one parent was interested in institutionalization. Nine mothers reported being able to talk over problems with their husbands; two were classified "unknown" in this category. Ten reported a good marital relationship; one was classified as "unknown." The mothers were satisfied for the most part with the services rendered and felt that they alleviated their problems. The types of persons that influenced were again the physician in eleven cases, although these mothers also reported others as assisting them in coming to a decision; nurse was mentioned four times, and a friend, a nursery school teacher, and the church (a Sister) were each mentioned once in addition to the physician. The pattern of this class of mothers then seemed to be more stability in relations, ability to cope with their problems, and reliance in medical advice, with some additional advice which helped bring them to the CSRC.

The one parent in the upper-middle-class category could not provide an adequate sample of this class, therefore, although this family is included in the table, no conclusions were reached regarding the factors listed.

Religion and Ethnicity. The data were analyzed to see if there were any correlations with religion or ethnic groups in the way families were able to cope with the child, in their feeling of acceptance, institutionalization, relationship, satisfaction with service, and so forth; but no such correlation appeared. It would seem, therefore, that any differences that exist in regard to these aspects of the problem are related more to socioeconomic status than to religion or ethnic group.

Coping Ability and Age. The data did indicate, however, that the age of the mother is a factor in coping ability. Of seven Group II mothers, for example, six indicated that they were able to cope with the retardate, and only one of the six was over the age of the one mother "unable" so to cope. The mother "unable" to cope was forty-two, and the one mother older in the "able" group was 43.7 years of age. The average age of the six mothers was 35.9 years of age or 6.3 years younger than the one "unable" mother.

In the study referred to earlier by Howard E. Freeman, he points to the importance of education and age as the two variables that correlate with mental illness attitudes.[3] Our sample was too small for quantitative analysis and was directed at reported behavior, yet the indication was quite strong in support of a similar correlation regarding age; that the younger mothers were better able to cope with their retarded children.[4] Regarding education, the limited knowledge of the last grade completed

---

[3] Freeman, *op. cit.*, p. 59.

[4] Attention is called to the fact that although Freeman's analysis was in terms of attitudes, the close association between attitudes and actual behavior is recognized as having a bearing on the present study in which all data were collected on the level of reported behavior.

was insufficient to make any judgment of the effect of education on coping ability. Perhaps a later study of a quantitative nature might examine the age and education factors as important variables in the coping ability of mothers with retarded children, and be able to report definitive results.

Analysis of the occupation of the father, and the mother's ability to manage in respect to some selected factors. Analysis of the possible correlation between the occupation of the fathers,[5] and any differences in the handling of the retardate as reported by the mother did not result in any significantly different patterns from those already described. The analysis examined the following factors in relation to blue collar versus white collar workers: coping ability; acceptance of the child, interest in institutionalization; ability of parents to talk over problems; parent relationships; satisfaction regarding services rendered; whether services alleviated problems, and types of persons having influence with the mothers.

Of the twenty-four families, eighteen were classified as blue collar and six as white collar. The reported actions of the mothers in terms of the factors listed above seemed not to center on occupation differences, but around the possible clue that hyperactivity, in the case of severe retardation, is more apt to be related to the parents' inability to cope with the child and to desire institutionalization. All other relationships in regard to the other factors seemed to exhibit the same patterns as previously mentioned. The blue collar families reporting themselves as unable to cope, for example, had children with the following diagnosis and conditions: (a) Microcephalic, hyperactive with emotional involvement; (b) Demyelinating disease of the central nervous system, and (c) Mongoloid, IQ under 20, unable to care for personal needs, nine years of age. The one white collar family unable to manage had a Cretin who was extremely hyperactive and at times completely beyond the family's control.

It would seem that both white and blue collar families, regard-

------

[5] The occupation breakdown was made on the rough designation of "blue" versus "white" collar using the Warner classification found in Table VI. Professional, clerks, and kindred workers were classed as white collar; manual workers, protective and service workers as blue collar.

less of the severity of the retardation, are less likely to want to keep the child at home if hyperactivity is one of the problems. Families unable to cope with the child found that tranquilizers were ineffective. (A significant number of parents had the same problem regarding the effectiveness of tranquilizers, but only in those cases where the child was extremely hyperactive did this become a problem.)

Education and the Mothers' Ability to Manage or Cope with the Retardate. A three-way split of the mothers was made according to education: eighth grade or less; ninth to twelfth grades, and, more than twelve grades. In respect to the same factors listed above, there were no significant differences which could be attributed to differences in education. A common assumption that mothers with less education might turn to friends and relatives for information on what to do with their retarded children did not prove to be the case. Of the seven mothers with eighth grade education or less, all relied on medical advice in respect to getting services for their children. Only in one case was the referral to a clinic made by a public health nurse without any other medical assistance. Of the eleven mothers with ninth to twelfth grade education, there was some indication of dependence on others but this was always in addition to medical advice, which again shows up as the most frequent source. The six mothers with more than twelfth grade education consistently used medical advice regarding services. In respect to the other factors listed, no different patterns emerged.

PATHS TO CONSULTATION

An analysis of the paths to consultation and action seems to indicate that, regardless of socioeconomic class, all of the mothers seemed to receive medical advice and help for their retarded children at a much earlier age than might have been expected. Although this sample had only five cases in the lower-lower-economic group, the average age at which the patient was seen by some medical service, that is either a doctor or a public health nurse, was 12.2 months. In contrast, the seven cases of our sample which belonged to the upper-lower group reached the doctor or nurse at the age of 24.6 months. This leads to the question as to whether or not the very lowest economic group may well be able to receive services because society has some concern in offering such services to this group. None of the mothers reported themselves as reluctant to seek medical advice or service. Without any exceptions, all mothers reported that they would seek medical help for the children in preference to any help, professional or nonprofessional, that might be available in the area. The lower-middle-class mothers, of which there were eleven in this sample, received their first tangible help when the patient was 22.1 months old. These mothers seemed to have a preponderance of referrals from the doctor to the Children's Hospital Medical Center in Boston. This raised the question as to whether or not the doctors were reluctant to make a quick referral to the CSRC. To find the answer, all referrals to Children's Hospital Medical Center were checked for the date that the patient was first seen. In all cases except one it was found to be prior to the opening of the CSRC, which accepted its first case in October, 1957. Unfortunately, the impression held by the staff of the CSRC that the doctors do not make quick referrals to it, except in unmistakable cases of retardation, cannot be confirmed at the moment because the Cambridge agency is still too new. Hopefully, at some later date this assumption may be either verified or discarded. Certainly, however, it is reasonable to assume that, except in obvious cases, a doctor would be reluctant to send the mother and the child to an agency that has the word "retarded" in its title and would be more inclined to send them to a hospital such as the Massachusetts General or the Children's Hospital Medical Center where stigmatization is less likely.

"Contrast" Group. Realizing that the sample was biased in favor of those who had already come to receive service, an attempt was made to locate other cases of mentally retarded children whose parents had not sought the services of the CSRC. The nearby Walter E. Fernald State School records were examined to locate any cases that had bypassed the CSRC and come directly to the school. Of the 1,187 out-patient records examined, only two cases were found that fulfilled all the criteria of our sample (brain damage, IQ of 50 or less, under ten years of age, and *residents of Cambridge*). Of the children in resi-

dence, there were three who fitted the above criteria at the time of admission. Two of these were doctors' children, and it can be assumed that these men made their own decision without recourse to any community social agency. The third, a child of a parent who had only recently come to Cambridge, had suffered severe development anomalies due to German Measles. The child suffered from deafness, spastic tetraplegia, a congenital cataract and optic atrophy. The attending physician had very strongly urged that the mother apply for the child's admission to the Fernald School and, in fact, had aided personally in the application.

Of the two children seen in the out-patient division, one of them died prior to the interview with the parents. In this case the parents were of upper-class socioeconomic status and relied entirely on the medical advice of their physician, who had not referred them to the CSRC, probably because the child was severely retarded due to brain damage at birth. The second child at the out-patient division subsequently moved from the Cambridge area, and it proved impossible to trace that particular family.

Aside from these five cases, it would seem that most of the families with a retarded child subsequent to the opening of the CSRC in the fall of 1957 did come to the Cambridge agency for help. Again this is not to say that a number of children were not seen by other services, such as the Children's Medical Center or the Massachusetts General Hospital, but as far as can be ascertained, once the clinic was in operation for a period of at least six to eight months, the number of cases that were referred there indicate quite markedly that the people of Cambridge have been utilizing the service extensively.

The only question that remained unresolved relates to the upper and upper-middle-class families in Cambridge. Since these families did not show up in the sample and since discussions with physicians and school people did not help locate cases, it was assumed that these families made direct contact with private or state schools that serve the retarded and placed the child themselves rather than through a service such as the CSRC. One of the mothers in the contrast group, the wife of the local physician, told the interviewer that she thought "services like the CSRC are for poor people, and we can afford to take care of our own problems."

Chapter V

THE SERVICES OF THE CLINIC

IT WAS INTERESTING to note that of the twenty-four families in the sample, fifteen came to the clinic asking for a nursery school experience for the child. Four of the families were not offered this service, for one reason or another—in most cases, the child was not ready, not toilet-trained, or had some physical handicap as in the case of the one paraplegic. In almost every case where this service was offered, the mothers claimed that it was a great help to the children and also gave them time to do some of the housework or to get out and visit, to see the neighbors, and so forth. The second most desired service for the child was speech therapy. In many cases, the mothers felt that if only the child could be taught to speak, he would be cured. Although only nine of the twenty-four mothers specifically asked for speech therapy for their children when they came to CSRC, almost every mother felt it to be necessary, believing that if such speech training could be given, the patient would improve.

Consultation and evaluation services were given in almost every case. Twenty-one of them are recorded as having had such evaluation and diagnosis. In several of the cases there was no such record because the evaluation and diagnosis had been given by some prior agency and the parents needed only further help or treatment, nursery school or speech therapy, as the case might be. It is interesting to note that only fifteen of the twenty-four mothers are reported as having come to the clinic for consultation and evaluation. This is the same number that came because they wanted "a nursery school." The question rises, then, as to the mothers' motivation in coming to a service such as the CSRC and whether, in effect, they do not come because of some physical service such as a nursery school or speech therapy class which they believe can be given. In other words, perhaps the average mother can see a service for her child only in concrete terms, whereas a professional may think in terms of evaluation and diagnosis.

Home training service rendered by the CSRC was asked for by only five of the twenty--four mothers. However, this service was offered in nineteen cases and accepted in every one. No mother was recorded as having rejected this service or the public health nurse who came into the home on a more or less regular basis. There were some cases where the nurse visited every week when that seemed indicated. In other cases, the nurse went less frequently, but, without any exception, the mothers indicated that this home visiting, or home training, as the public health nurse saw it, was of special help not only to the child but to the mother.

Also, the mothers said that the nurse's visits were extremely helpful because they gave the mothers someone to talk to who understood their problems. The mothers apparently felt that the nurse could identify herself with them and really understood them. The fact that the nurse visited in the home and on a fairly regular basis established a good relationship. In ten out of the twenty-four cases, the mothers specifically mentioned that *talking* with the nurse was a great help to them, although the nurse performed many other functions. In this connection it is worth noting that no visit of the nurse or any service was rejected by the mothers, but that in four situations where case work was indicated, three of the four mothers rejected it saying they "didn't need it." In addition, there were four instances where case work was indicated as a needed service, but where after discussion at case conference and at the recommendation of the case worker, the decision was made not to offer it.

The interviews brought out the following problems in relation to the available case work services: (a) The mothers usually regarded the case worker as the intake person who "asks you a lot of questions"; (b) as may be seen from the previous statement, the role of the case worker was not clear in the mothers' minds; (c) the case worker was not able to establish the kind of friendly and helpful relationship which the nurse established through her home visits. In the few instances where the case worker had maintained a home visit schedule with mothers that needed her services, a more favorable attitude on their part was noticeable, and (d) mothers that need the service are apt to reject it on the basis that "going to the office and talking with a social worker isn't going to help you." The meaning of this statement and other comments by mothers regarding social case work will be examined in greater detail later.

Some Illustrative Cases. By random selection, three cases were pulled from the files to illustrate the kinds of services for which mothers came to CSRC and the kinds of services they received.

Mrs. M. came for nursery school, speech therapy, and consultation. She was offered the nursery school service, the consultation service, and home training service. The speech therapy was not offered because at the time only limited service was available and the staff of the clinic did not feel they could deal adequately with the needs of the patient. The other services were rendered and accepted with good results. In addition, the home training service was found to be worthwhile and was accepted. An additional benefit was discovered in that the mother gained a great deal from her talks with the nursery school teachers. She reported that this was extremely valuable to her, not only in giving her a better insight into her problems but because she had someone to talk with who understood the problems of mental retardation.

Mrs. S. Mrs. S. was interested in nursery school, speech therapy, consultation, and glasses for the patient. She was offered and accepted all these services. In addition, she received the services of the public health nurse who visited the home on a regular basis and helped with other problems related to the husband's illness. The study brought out the fact that these visits by the public health nurse were an integral part of the entire service provided by the CSRC and served a very important part of the help offered to this family.

Mrs. L. Mrs. L. came to the Cambridge Service wanting nursery school and help in the home training of her child. These two services were offered and rendered, and were well accepted by the client. In addition, she was offered and accepted consultation and evaluation services and visits from the public health nurse. In respect to the help that this mother received, she told the interviewer, "They are all so nice and have been a great help to me. I would really have been ready for the asylum if it hadn't been for the Cambridge Service and the nursery school." This mother mentioned particularly the help that she had had from the public health nurse, although other staff members were also mentioned favorably.

WHAT SERVICES ARE USED BY THE MOTHERS?

The services used by the mothers which they reported as having the most meaning and value to them were the nursery school and the public health nurse home visits. These two services are not necessarily the most significant, but they are the ones reported most often by the mothers. After some probing on the part of the interviewer as to other services received and their value, some mothers did say that they were able to get a definitive answer in respect to a diagnosis and evaluation of their child, while others said nothing about diagnosis or evaluation even under a probe. It did not seem important to them. The value of this latter service, however, cannot be overlooked even in cases where the mother already knew beyond doubt that her child was mentally retarded. The fact that the CSRC staff members are understanding and able to establish warm, friendly relations with the mothers means that the services given and received had a value far beyond the mere confirmation of the original diagnosis. Several mothers mentioned their relief in being able to talk with someone. This may seem strange or contradictory since the mother's responses to the specific question "What helps?" were usually in terms of some physical service. The writer assumes, however, that average mothers would be inclined to report obvious services. That talking out their problems did help them was reflected in comments previously quoted; but lacking was the perception that talking to staff (and staff listening) was a part of the *service rendered* which they as mothers *used*. A number of the mothers, for example, remarked regarding the nursery school, "The teachers are so friendly you feel you can talk with them about your problems—they really understand." Regarding parents' meetings some mothers said, "I wish I could get out to some of those meetings—it sure helps to talk with other parents who are in the same boat."

SERVICES MOTHERS REPORT AS ALLEVIATING OR MODIFYING THEIR PROBLEMS

The anaylsis separated the help to the child according to whether it related to medical or to nonmedical aspects, and then the help to the parents on the same basis. As to the children, it was found that the services reported by the parents as being "most helpful" in modifying problems were, *first,* the medical services rendered by the Cambridge Service (especially prescription of tranquilizers, eye glasses and other prostheses, vitamin and diet therapy); *second,* the nursery school, and, *third* the home training and public health nurse visits to the home. The last two services ranked the same in interest as far as the parents were concerned. A curious fact emerged from the remarks by the parents about the nursery school. A number of times they mentioned that better adjustment had been achieved. In nine out of the ten cases reported, the nursery school was credited with exerting a nonmedical or non physical influence on the child in making him better adjusted and able to get along socially with his peers. On the other hand, the mothers who spoke of the visits of the public health nurse did not always mention the nonphysical help that the nurse gave to the patient and the mother by her visits, but instead always equated the nurse's visits with physical care.

In respect to the parents, the service mentioned most often as helping to alleviate or modify problems was the home training visits of the public health nurse, with "talking to the staff at CSRC" following closely. In other words, the mothers saw the visits of the public health nurse and talking to the staff as being of help to them personally on a nonphysical basis and more related to emotional release, while the work of the public health nurse, as far as the child was concerned, was related more to a physical help.

A few cases will illustrate how helpful the parents found the services.

Mrs. X. A mother with a high school and some business education, had come to CSRC with a diagnosis for her child. She was interested in obtaining schooling for him and asked for information in regard to schools. This was given her with the result that not only was she herself helped but also the child in respect to his social adjustment. The mother also reported that the public health nurse and the staff took the time to talk with her and that this meant a great deal to her.

Mrs J. This mother, a high school graduate, came to the CSRC for medical help and speech therapy for her child. She reported that both of these services were rendered, and alleviated in great measure some of the child's problems. In addition, the mother said that talking with the public health nurse, the doctor on the staff, and the nursery school teacher in charge was a great "relief" to her.

Mrs. R. A mother with a ninth grade education, she reported that the medical and psychological services given by the CSRC aided the child in functioning better. The mother also stated that the nursery school was a definite help to him. These services to the child were reported as having assisted on a medical or physical basis. With respect to the mother herself, the public health nurse's help rested not only on a physical but also on a nonphysical basis. The case worker and the public health nurse, in their visits to the home, talked with her about her problems, all of which relieved her greatly, both mentally and emotionally.

Mrs. Q. A mother with a tenth grade education, she also spoke of the medical service and public health nurse as the services of most help to the child on a physical basis. For herself, she mentioned the visits of the public health nurse as being most helpful. This mother, who had moved to the Cambridge area from one of the southern states, is in a rather desperate economic situation. She lacked furniture, food, and so forth. These were taken care of by the public health nurse and the case worker together. The mother reported, "It was a relief to me to have some of the things I needed and to know that someone cared enough to help."

It may be seen from these four cases that, normally speaking, the mothers see the services rendered to the child as helping to alleviate the problems on a medical or physical basis, but rarely mentioned the possibility that they may also have been modified on a nonmedical or nonphysical basis.

WHAT THE RECORDS SHOW

The case records were examined to (a) verify impressions of the family gained by the interviewer; (b) examine the services reported as helpful versus the record of services given, and (c) examine the influences on the mothers during the preclient phase leading up to their perceptions of the problem at time of intake.

Before undertaking the examination, the author checked to see what types of information were available in the case records kept by the CSRC. First, a general information form contained the following: Referral source, date of application, case number. Birth dates of all members of the family. Education of all members of the family. Marital information, religion, birthplace of members. Other relatives in the household. Nonrelatives in the household. Housing information. Occupation and income. Ethnic group, language spoken. Whether parents are members of a group for retarded. Child discussed with anyone else. Previous medical care. Permission to contact medical and other agencies.

Second, a work-up folder held medical, social work, psychological testing, public health nurse data and other relevant data, if any, from referral sources. Third, the case conference evaluation which recorded the decisions of the staff regarding the treatment plan agreed upon. Fourth, running accounts were given of contacts, interviews, and home visits by the staff.

Impressions of the Family. The examinations of the records took place after the interviews. With the exception of a very few cases the impressions gained by the interviewer in his home visit regarding socioeconomic status, marital accord, and care of the children coincided with the case records. Differences were most notable in the mother's expectations of the retardate. In almost all cases, these were far higher than the case record suggested regarding the child's level of functioning. Perhaps professionals, because they do leave out value judgments, strike (unintentionally) a note of gloom that often is not shared by the mothers. Two extreme cases will point up this tendency:

Mrs. S. and her husband were married late in life and decided on adoption of a child as the best thing for them. Arrangements were made with a church-sponsored agency and a newborn child was given to Mr. and Mrs. S. by the agency. Almost at once, however, the foster mother noticed that the child was not well and took her back to the hospital for examination. The child was kept by the hospital, and the agency notified the adoptive parents-to-be that the child was diagnosed as mentally retarded, probably due to brain injury, had multiple physical anomalies and a congenital heart defect. They therefore expressed their decision not to release the child for adoption and advised Mr. and Mrs. S. to wait for another child.

One would assume that, given such a shocking description of a child not yet a week old, even the child's parents would hesitate to take him into the home. In this case, as potential adoptive parents, Mr. and Mrs. S. had every reason to drop their interest in this child and wait for another (something the natural mother could not very well do!). Instead, they fought to keep the child and began a long, up-hill fight to convince the agency, the hospital, the church, and the doctors that they were doing the right thing.

The hospital evaluation was that the child would never have an IQ above 20 and would almost surely be a "vegetable." Immediate institutionalization was recommended. Mr. and Mrs. S. refused to believe that the evaluation really indicated the patient's potential. They decided to do all they could to improve her functioning and at least bring her up to the highest level of which she was capable.

Today, at eight years of age, this child is functioning almost normally in many respects, is able to dress herself, feed herself, is toilet-trained, and is going to a parochial school. She is exhibiting the possibility of reaching an IQ in the sixties (according to the staff psychologist). Both Mr. and Mrs. S. spend a great deal of time with the child and give her loving and patient care. The response has been remarkable.

The criticism of the above case may be that, after all, this just proves that the child was not really retarded. In answer, we would have to say that the records were detailed and complete. The child was suffering from multiple problems of which brain damage was only one. The adoptive parents simply did not give up.

The "S" family is Roman Catholic, lower-middle class, and with no other children.

Mr. and Mrs. G. were told the night their son "F" was born that he was brain damaged due to difficulty with the placenta at birth and consequent lack of oxygen for the child. The mother refused to believe that there was anything wrong with "F" and treated him just as she treated the rest of her children. At six or seven months, however, the mother first began to wonder if the physician might have been right about the diagnosis. However, even after taking the patient back for observation, the mother did not accept unquestionably the diagnosis. Instead, the record quotes her as saying, "I always thought that "F" would disprove the doctor's diagnosis."

This patient when seen by the CSRC, was classified as spastic paraplegic, with a chronological age of seven and functioning at a two-year-old level. The psychologist could not administer tests but had to guess at the level of functioning.

The mother works intensively with the patient and has so improved his physical functioning that she hopes he will soon be able to walk with the aid of crutches.

The "G" family is Protestant, lower-middle-class, and has a total of six children.

The point in emphasizing these two families is that they dramatize what seems to be prevalent with all of the mothers, to a greater or lesser degree: they have tremendous faith that they can improve their children's functioning. Although all the mothers seemed to exhibit this trait to some degree, there was one pattern that seemed recurrent. Some mothers intellectually and emotionally accepted the diagnosis but kept working with the patient because, in reality, they rejected the prognosis. Other mothers intellectually accepted the diagnosis but kept fighting it emotionally. The latter cases were harder on the mothers because in fighting the diagnosis they also by implication rejected the prognosis. They exhibited "nervousness" and general unhappiness with the situation in which they found themselves.

Since this study was not designed to explore the psychological implications of a tendency such as the one noted above, we can only call attention to this difference in perception with the hope that clinic staff and other researchers may examine its implications further.

SERVICES OFFERED

In regard to the actual services performed by the CSRC, the one conspicuous discrepancy was between what the mothers reported as "being of most help" and the treatment plan outlined by the staff. The mothers, for example, were highly complimentary and commended the CSRC for the service of the public health nurse who visited them regularly. The mothers saw the public health nurse as a "friendly person" with whom you could talk over your problems and who "understood." The mothers never forgot the nurse's professional capacity, however, and asked and expected to receive advice on the care and development of the retardate and other family members. The nurse frequently was called upon to make referrals to other agencies or staff members. As far as the mothers were concerned, the public health nurse then was very strongly identified as *the* important service. In contrast to this very strong view held by the mothers, the CSRC case records indicate a whole gamut of services of which the public health nurse is only one—although a very important one.

Another service, mentioned about as often as the public health nurse, was the nursery school. Again, granting that this is an important service, one wonders why mothers seemed to have it uppermost in their thoughts. Why didn't they mention the psychologist or the physician more often? These latter two services are most important in providing data for proper evaluation of the child. Yet, unless probed for further information as to "what else helped," the mothers most often mentioned only the nurse, the nursery school, and, further down the list, the speech therapist. Perhaps the services of the psychologist and the physician are "taken for granted." Perhaps if the interviewer had presented the mothers with a list of all the services rendered the mothers might have given preference to some of the other services.

The fact that the mothers were *not* directed in any way by the interviewer resulted in their reporting what was uppermost in their minds; the two services most personally theirs. We may assume, therefore, that a mother perceives of services as being "most helpful" if they in some way aid her personally: the public health nurse relieves some of her tensions and gives practical help with the children; the nursery school relieves her of the care of the child for a few hours and gives her a chance to take care of her personal needs, to do extra work around the house, or to do the marketing. This need, then, which is being met by these two services is important and perhaps calls for further examination. Persons responsible for the administration of services for the retarded might find this area a fruitful one for research. The present study can at least call attention to that fact and suggest that any service which affects the mothers as personally as the two mentioned should be analyzed carefully so that the processes involved may be truly understood.

Case Work. In regard to the services of the social worker, several important facts developed from comparison of the interview data with the case records. First, the case worker is not usually perceived by the mothers as a "help." Only three mothers mentioned her as someone they really knew, although all twenty-four had an intake interview and one or more subsequent interviews. The mothers thought of these as being information-giving sessions to answer some need of the CSRC. Only two mothers definitely mentioned the social worker as "helping" them. This should not be construed to mean that because the mothers failed to mention the case worker that the service is unimportant or not needed, but that in the sample studied various factors were at work to mitigate its importance in the mothers' minds.

The case records revealed that of the four mothers who had been "offered" case work services only one accepted. The other three rejected it as a service for themselves or their families. In addition to the above four mothers, there were four others who were seen as "needing case work services," but the staff decision recorded that, "Case work was not offered," because the mother was unable to benefit, resisted help, was too disturbed, or was not properly motivated.

The present study was not designed to study the implications of this inconsistency and to ask the question, "Why is it that a helping service such as social case work is not perceived that way by the mothers?" But even if we did not study the question, we can speculate on a few possibilities: (a) that the sample under consideration is not truly representative of the total population (in a statistical sense); (b) that there are class differences mitigating against the use of case work services, (the sample is composed almost wholly of blue collar workers); (c) that the families have problems that do not require the skilled services of a case worker, and (d) that the staff and case worker were more concerned with other cases in greater need of service.

In regard to the above question, the administration of an agency needs to ask about its casework services: (a) What *are* the case work services that families need which we can provide (services that include intake; family problem diagnosis; psychodynamic implications, and individual or group therapy)? (b) Are these case work services possible for us with the staff and time available? (c) If we do not provide these services, is there another agency that can do so? (d) What are the possible consequences of our meeting or failing to meet these needs?[1]

The above suggests that any agency aiming to assist families with retarded children must be prepared to offer the services that help meet the mother's deep psychological and emotional needs as well as to take care of the physical and psychological needs of

---

[1] See William R. Vath: School for forgotten children. *Today's Health,* 39:66 July, 1961, in which he discusses the role of the social worker at the Shield of David Institute for Retarded Children in New York City. Casework is a condition of the child's attendance at the Institute's school—the caseworker's job: to interpret to the parents their contribution to the child's development or retardation; to get acceptance of the fact that mental retardation is a family situation which must be met with the personality, strengths, and resources which any problem in living must be met; to help the family achieve maximum mental health; to interpret the school staff's general thinking and evaluation of the child's capacity, and to report to the staff the conditions in each child's home and changes in parents' attitudes.

the retardate. This calls attention to the one factor that may be most difficult to deal with and for which assignment of personnel may also be most difficult. What helps in one case because of warm friendly relationships established by a public health nurse, social worker, physician, or psychologist, may not work in another case because of personality factors beyond the reach of the administration. The question: "Whose function is it to do so and so," may very well have to be answered with another question: "Who has, or can establish quickly, the best relationship?"

The Preclient Phase. This particular period has been variously labeled the "decision-making process" or the "preclient phase," or the "paths to . . ." by various writers.[2] Its importance rests on the need to know (a) who the preclient relies upon for definition of the problem; (b) in going to an agency—who or what helps—hinders, and (c) what are the preclient's perceptions of the problem (or problems) at the time of intake. The case records and the interview data will be contrasted in the examination of these three questions.

In general we can say that contrary to some assumptions, the mothers rely on physicians to define the possibility of retardation. The records often indicate the "referral source" as a public health nurse or as a "self-referral," but checking further one almost always finds that the mother saw a physician first[3] and from him received a fairly clear notion that her child was retarded. Mothers, however, tend to want this first diagnosis reaffirmed. This accounts for the so-called "shopping around" in which mothers may see an average of two or three more specialists or other sources before coming to believe that their children are

---

[2] David Landy, *op. cit.*, p. 127. See John A. Clausen and Marion Radke Yarrow: Paths to the mental hospital. *The Journal of Social Issues,* 11:25, No. 4, 1955. See also August B. Hollingshead and Frederick C. Redlich: Paths to the psychiatrist. *Social Class and Mental Illness.* New York, John Wiley and Sons, Inc., p. 171. Clausen and Yarrow, for example ask the following questions: "Who defines and who assists in defining the nature of the patient's difficulty? What persons, lay or professional, enter into the process of dealing with the patient and getting him to treatment? What persons, beliefs, or circumstances either facilitate or hinder effective action . . .?"

[3] Levinson and Bigler support the conclusion that ". . . the physician is the one who is usually called upon to decide whether the child is retarded." See Levinson and Bigler, *op. cit.*, p. 12.

really retarded and that they themselves must begin to care for them on that level. An example of this pattern is Mrs. X:

> Interviewer: This mother reported, "She was my first child and I didn't know very much about children, but I did think that she was a baby for too long a period, so I asked the doctor if anything was wrong." The mother took the child regularly to her pediatrician who kept her informed in detail through long memoranda about the child's development. This child, then, was seen regularly by the pediatrician from the time of birth. It was not until the patient was close to four years of age that the doctor finally told the mother he too was concerned about the possibility of retardation. The pediatrician then made a referral to the Children's Medical Center. The mother took the patient to the CMC for a full year before the diagnosis of retardation was made.
>
> Following this experience, the patient, now five years of age, was taken by the mother to the nearest kindergarten at the September school opening. The mother told the school the diagnosis of retardation. The child was accepted but after a few months the school could not tolerate the abnormal behavior and requested that the child be removed. Another school (a private one) was tried and then the following year the mother again enrolled the patient in the public kindergarten. The same pattern of abnormal behavior again brought a request to remove the child, but this time the public health nurse came to the home to explain the situation and to talk to the mother about taking the child to the CSRC. On the face sheet of the agency, the referral source is listed as, the public health nurse.

From the above condensed version of the interview and the case records one can see the importance of looking at the entire clinical record of the patient in order to determine "who influences the mother to come to an agency." In this case, as in many others in the sample, the mother had had many contacts prior to going to the CSRC. Almost without fail these medical advisors (a pediatrician, family doctor, clinic doctor, or nurse) had given a pretty fair indication (or in some cases a definite diagnosis) of retardation. In other words, the mothers *knew.* When they came to the CSRC they also knew that this was the "end of the line." Only a few mothers in the sample admitted having looked elsewhere after having come to the CSRC and even they did not pursue these possibilities to any extent.

The case records and the interviewer's data were in agreement that the mothers did not rely on relatives, neighbors, friends, clergy, or other nonmedical professionals in the decision to take the child for early examination and for later treatment at a clinic. Here again, some assumptions to the contrary, the mother may have discussed her child with some of these persons but with the following typical comments resulting:

> In regard to relatives: "They don't know anything about retardation, so why waste your time."
>
> "They feel sorry for you. They don't know really what to say. Sometimes you think they feel awkward—like somebody died or something."
>
> In regard to friends and neighbors: "They mean well, but they tell you, 'God gave you this cross to bear and there's nothing you can do about it.' Boy, did I tell one of my neighbors off one day when she gave me that stuff. I told her it was in the genes and not to blame God."
>
> In regard to the clergy: "No, I never discussed my child with the priest. This is a medical problem and it's no use discussing it with them." (This viewpoint, incidentally, was expressed by almost every Roman Catholic family. The clergy were seen as important only in respect to the religious instruction of the retardate.)

Naturally, not all families made the same comments. There were two or three mothers who expressed fondness for their relatives and the latter's "understanding" of a difficult situation. One mother mentioned her sister-in-law as being helpful, willing to baby-sit on occasion, and always cutting out "news items for me to read." On the whole, however, the impression given above is substantially correct, that the mothers do not rely on such nonmedical persons to persuade them to take their children for treatment.

Our present question deals with the next phase—going to the agency—who or what helps or hinders. After the initial definition of the problem, the mothers began a pattern of "shopping around" as it has been called by a number of writers. This phase may also be called the "period of doubt" because in essence what happens is that the mother is seeking confirmation, or hopefully, rejection of the diagnosis. The case records substantiated the interviewer's data in this respect. Most mothers averaged at least two contacts, and some three, with other "sources" before going to the CSRC. The pattern of help-seeking was usually as follows: (a) First, the child was taken to a physician, who then referred the matter directly to the Children's Medical Center (CMC), or the Massachusetts General Hospital, or "suggested" that the mothers take the child to a clinic; (b) the mothers then went to the CMC or some other hospital for an evaluation of their child, a process that might take six or eight weeks or as long as a year, and finally (c) they were referred or made a "self-referral" to the CSRC.

Because of the smallness of the sample and the possibility that other factors might be operative, it was difficult to generalize about possible differences due to social class. Attention, however, should be directed to differences in the number and type of contacts prior to coming to the CSRC between the lower-class-group and the lower-middle-class.

The lower-lower and the upper-lower-class sample together consisted of twelve cases; five in the former and seven in the latter. The lower-lower-group followed the usual pattern (four out of five) and went to a physician for the first contact. The second and subsequent contacts, if any, seemed to be more diverse than the pattern found in the lower-middle-class group. In two cases, a nurse was the person who helped the mothers get to the agency; in another case, the Boston Association for Retarded Children (the mother had called there and asked for help); and two cases are listed as "self-referrals" (one of these had previously been given a diagnosis of retardation from a "Well Baby Clinic" and CMC; the other had been to CMC and to Wrentham State School). The upper-lower-group showed a similar pattern of a nurse, a friend, a relative, or a neighbor as the person who had also helped get the mother to the CSRC.

In the lower-middle-class group nine out of eleven mothers

were either referred directly from the CMC or made a "self-referral" to the CSRC after having been at the CMC. All prior contacts leading to the CSRC were medical. The significant difference seemed to be the total absence of nonmedical persons influencing this group to come to the agency. After the definition of the problem by a physician, the next step for this group was a more elaborate evaluation by the CMC and then a direct referral through the social worker of the CMC to the CSRC or a "self-referral" (although every "self-referral" had already received a complete evaluation on the child). Directly or indirectly then, a medical service helped the mother make up her mind to take the retardate to the CSRC. In nine of the eleven cases it was the CMC, and in the other two cases a public health nurse.

The above paragraphs dealt with "who" helped to bring the mother to the agency. The question of "what" helped may be more difficult to answer in light of the size of the sample. Analysis of the possible effect of the following variables, age of retardate at intake, the mother's health, the mother's age, total number of children in the family, and religion, indicates differences that would bear further investigation.

The lower-lower class group (five cases) showed an average age for the mothers of 28.7 years; had a total of 5.2 children per family; brought the children to the CSRC at an average age of 52.1 months, and were divided religiously into three Roman Catholic and two Protestant families. The upper-lower-class group (seven cases) showed an average age for the mothers of 35.3 years; had a total of 3.1 children per family; brought the children to the CSRC at an average age of 43.0 months, and included six Roman Catholic families and one Protestant.

The lower-middle-class group (eleven cases) showed an average age for the mothers of 36.6 years; had a total of 3.4 children per family; brought the child to the CSRC at an average age of 52.4 months, and was made up of ten Roman Catholic and one Protestant family.

The direction is made clearer (although no generalization is intended or implied) if the figures for the upper-lower and the lower-middle-class are combined. The indication then is that the mothers of these groups bring their children in to the CSRC at an earlier age (48.7 months) in contrast to the lower-lower-class group of 52.1 months; that they have an average of two children fewer per family, and that they themselves are about seven years older. Neither religion nor the health of the mother seemed correlated with bringing the retardate to the clinic in any of the class categories.

Since the interview analysis (in the previous chapter) showed that the lower-lower-class mothers received medical service for their retarded children at an earlier age (12.2 months) than other class groups (upper-lower, 24.6 and lower- middle, 22.1), it seems obvious that something is operating to cause lower-lower-class mothers to wait longer before taking their retardate to the CSRC although advised of the condition at an earlier period. Since these same families are also the larger ones, could it be that having larger families tends to immobilize the mothers' regard for possible action?

In summary, it is evident that at least three factors seem to relate to the question "What helps (or hinders) the mother in getting to an agency?" (a) the age of the mother; (b) the size of the family, and (c) the socioeconomic status. Precisely how these factors influence the mother cannot be pinpointed since a much larger sample would be necessary in order to validate any causal relationship. At this point it is only possible to call attention to the need for further study.

What were the mothers' perceptions of the problem (or problems) at the time of intake? In almost every instance the mothers were aware that the problem was one of retardation before they went to the CSRC. The case records show this agency as being the "end of the line" as regards evaluation and treatment; the mothers now perceived that theirs was not just a physical problem. In the first or second step of the help-seeking process, it will be recalled, the mothers still were hopeful that a physical fault would be causing the difficulty. An indication of this type of reasoning is the mothers' use of "cerebral palsy" to explain the child's retardation. Some mothers persisted in using this term even though that diagnosis had been ruled out by the physicians. Two possible explanations suggest themselves: (a) there is some hope in the mind of the mother that cerebral palsy can be "cured," and (b) the term "cp" has been publicized and connotes a physical condition which carries less stigma than a mental condition. However, by the time they have reached the CSRC, most of the mothers had realized that the problem was one of mental retardation. This does not necessarily mean that they had *accepted* the diagnosis, nor understood the degree of retardation, or the problems of the future and necessary treatment. By the time the mother came to the CSRC, the child was also older (an average of forty-six to fifty-two months), and the mother had had ample time to recognize hers as no ordinary problem.

Another pattern that seemed to emerge and was verified by the case records is that the mothers tended to think of mental retardation in terms of speech difficulty. Most of the mothers mentioned this problem at intake and seemed to equate this difficulty with the *reason* for the mental retardation. Perhaps they did not really think in terms of causal relationships, but the evidence certainly points to the concept that mental retardation is related to inability to talk. Typical of many mothers are Mrs. N. and Mrs. X:

> Interviewer: Mrs. N. brought her son "B" to the CSRC because her son could not talk. She said, "I don't know why the doctor asked me to bring him to a place for retarded children. His only problem is that he can't talk." The child (a Mongoloid, five years old at intake) was able to dress and feed himself, was completely ambulatory, and toilet-trained. "B" can say perhaps a dozen words, but has no real speech skills.
>
> Interviewer: Mrs. X. did not mention speech at the time of intake; instead she said she wanted information about schools. The interview, however, revealed that the mother's concern was in regard to speech. The patient, "O," was described by the mother as having, "a slurring speech so that many times you can't understand what she is trying to say; at other times, it is quite clear." (The patient was diagnosed, "moderate to severe retardation." Etiology: congenital cerebral defect.") Information regarding schooling was given the mother and some help in making application for private schooling. Significantly, the case conference records read, "Plan: (a) Try

to explain to the mother the significance of 'O's retardation; (b) study the effect of 'O' on sibling 'L'; (c) discuss with mother about joining a parents' group, and (d) see 'O' again in one year."

In the last case, particularly, one should note that the mother's perception of the problem was not at all the perception of the staff, and that the mother, perhaps unwittingly, masked her concern about speech in the intake interview. In the research interview the numerous references to the patient's speech difficulties revealed the mother's real concern. (Only one child in the sample of twenty-four had "normal" speech; nine had "below normal"; three, "very much below normal"; and eleven, "no speech" or "completely unintelligible.") In the light of the importance placed upon speech and intelligence in our society, the mothers' concern was understandable.

The evidence indicates that too often mothers bring to the initial intake interview a perception of mental retardation in which retardation is seen as being the result of the inability to speak. This suggests that a clinic staff needs to be aware of this perception and be prepared to deal with it when helping the mother understand the meaning of retardation.

Finally, the mothers saw themselves, generally, as having only one problem—the retardation of their children. At the intake interview the mother, and sometimes both parents if they came together for the interview, discussed the problem of their child in terms of retardation. The fact that the family often had multiple problems, of which retardation was only one, did not develop out of the first interview. The mothers often did not recognize their problem as a family one until much later, and only after considerable interpretation from one or more staff members. The crucially important element here is that the CSRC is organized around the concept of helping the whole family. This approach makes it easier for the staff to interpret the larger family needs to the mother and so to offer services which will be of real assistance.

Staff Consensus. In addition to the mothers' perceptions regarding mental retardation, this study also examines the services rendered by the staff. This involves two important areas of concern—the possible effect of staff consensus regarding diagnosis, treatment plan, and prognosis by (a) the educational orientation of the various disciplines represented by the staff members, and (b) staff biases and interpersonal dynamics.

One reason for examining consensus is that clinic programs such as the CSRC are relatively new and the "team" concept operative in these programs is relatively untried. Problems that exist or come into being as a result of this concept are often not identified or understood as problems which involve group dynamics. Indeed, the present study, because of its focus on other elements, can only call attention to the need for research regarding the problem of group dynamics in a clinical setting. As explained elsewhere (Chapter I), the CSRC, in common with about forty or more similar agencies throughout the country, employs a team of specialists whose responsibility is to see that services are rendered in line with the best thinking of a variety of disciplines. This requires a kind of orientation that perhaps few, if any, practitioners receive. The training of the physician, for example, is oriented towards his being the expert, the "authority figure,"[4] regarding illness. It is natural, therefore, for this attitude of authority to carry over into a clinic setting, especially one staffed by nonmedical personnel. How does this authority orientation affect the other members of the team and is there a possible effect on the clients? Schwartz, in a study of the decision-making process of various categories of personnel in a mental hospital, claims that there are important effects on the patients of ". . . the system and methods of distributing authority and responsibility . . ."[5] Even under the best of conditions, then, one might expect a certain tendency towards authoritarianism which could be detrimental to the team concept which envisions each professional member as having a meaningful voice. This is

---

[4] Leila Calhoun Deasy and Olive Westbrooke Quinn: The wife of the mental patient and the hospital psychiatrist. *The Journal of Social Issues, 11*:58, No. 4, 1955. Deasy and Quinn quote from Talcott Parsons, *The Social System*, in which the latter discusses the crucial aspects of the role of the doctor.

[5] Morris S. Schwartz: Social research in the mental hospital. *Social Perspectives on Behavior*, (Ed) Herman D. Stein and Richard A. Cloward, Glencoe, The Free Press, 1959, p. 593.

not the place to discuss the authoritarian versus the democratic roles which are involved, but only to point to the problem as one that confronts the administrator. The team concept brings together as equals in professional knowledge persons who previously have not necessarily been granted peer status, from a variety of professional disciplines, each with its own orientation.

Discussing one aspect of this problem, Edward Wellin theorizes that "contrasting professional orientations" provide a clue to differential approaches which contribute to the possibility of disagreements. These professional orientations he labels "individual-centered" and "group-centered."[6] His thesis is that the staff members of a clinic are basically oriented towards one or the other of these two concepts and that therein lies the possibility for disagreements or lack of consensus which occur from time to time.[7] The individual-centered orientation tends ". . . to eliminate nearly everything from consideration except a focus on diagnosis and the formulations of recommendations to the parents."[8] The group-centered orientation tends

> . . . to regard mental retardation as the index defect to the anticipated cluster of defects, not all of which may be necessarily related to mental deficit; it also means a readiness to regard the family as a whole and not the retarded child alone as the patient.[9]

These two concepts are presented as extremes, although in practice a staff member may alternate or vary his view of the client for one reason or another.

Wellin, a cultural anthropologist, noted that the social worker, psychologist, and psychiatrist "tended toward an individual

---

[6] Edward Wellin: Public and professional attitudes toward mental retardation. A presentation before the Public Health Nurses Section of the Forty-Second Biennial Convention of the American Nurses' Association, Miami Beach, Florida, May 2-6, 1960. This presently unpublished paper by Dr. Wellin confirms many of the writer's observations and impressions gathered from talking with various staff members of the CSRC, of which agency Dr. Wellin was study director during 1957-1958.

[7] Hollingshead and Redlich have pointed to the difference in psychiatric orientation as leading to dissimilar treatment, *op. cit.*, pp. 155-160.

[8] Wellin, *op. cit.*

[9] *Ibid.*

orientation"; while the public health nurse, nutritionist, and anthropologist "tended toward a group orientation." The pediatrician and nursery school teacher seemed not committed to either orientation and consequently moved from one to the other.[10]

At what point did the differences become most pronounced and turn into a lack of consensus, and around what problems? The writer's observation corroborates Wellin's that the case conference, a weekly meeting of the entire staff and interested persons, was the focal point for the disagreements that occurred. Not that all case conferences tend to end in disagreement, but that any disagreements will certainly be exposed at this time. Here we see most sharply differentiated the professional judgments growing out of differing interpretations of the data on the case under discussion. Although there was no way to obtain a scientific sampling of decisions made over the years, the writer again corroborates Wellin's observations that, "There were perhaps fewest conflicts over diagnostic evaluation as such. When disagreements did arise, they were usually in connection with everything else (i.e., case findings; recommendations to parents as to care, management, or special education; follow-up; etc.)."[11] These disagreements then are ascribed by Wellin to differences in orientation.

It is important to point out that some differences develop around diagnosis and the consequent treatment plan that are not necessarily fundamental to the individual-centered or group-centered orientation concepts. In a number of the cases examined there were at least four factors that had little or no direct bearing on orientation but nevertheless influenced the decision reached in the staff conference.[12] Those factors are (a) lack of clarity

---

[10] *Ibid.* Only the public health nurse who was one of Wellin's staff is still with the program. She gave the writer many valuable insights.

[11] *Ibid.*

[12] The four factors discussed were observed within the clinical setting of the CSRC. It is not implied that these are the only factors involved in interdisciplinary collaboration or communication. Indicative of reporting in this area of study is the work of Caudill and Roberts cited throughout this chapter. See also Margaret Barron Luszki: *Interdisciplinary Team Research: Methods and Problems.* Washington, National Training Laboratories, New York University Press, 1958, especially Chapter IV where she discusses differences of orientation of scientists and practitioners and differences due to stereotyped notions of research.

regarding etiology which resulted in differential diagnoses; (b)
lack of interest or desire to work with a particular family (i.e.,
the personal equation and "pseudoconsensus"); (c) rigidity in
holding to a treatment plan even if its effectiveness was questioned, and (d) bias (which may be traced to orientation in
some cases) that results in wanting to attack the "tangibles" in
the case of the public health nurse and the "intangibles" in the
case of the psychologist or case worker.

An example of lack of clarity regarding etiological factors as
the basic problem in lack of consensus is illustrated in the case
of the "I" family. The staff was divided on the diagnosis; the
psychologist said that the retardate was suffering from a severe
emotional trauma due to a skin condition and the subsequent
hospital care involved tying the patient's hands to the bed; the
pediatrician regarded the patient's behavior as symptomatic of
some organic defect. The staff lined up for and against these two
judgments. In the end the situation was diagnosed as organic
deficit, with strong emotional overlay. This kind of a decision involves strong differences in the treatment potential. If the staff
inclines towards the emotional factor in the diagnosis, then there
is apt to be a more optimistic approach to the patient with strong
emphasis on psychotherapy, social case work, and maximum goals.
If the staff inclines towards the organic interpretation, then there
is apt to be a much less optimistic atmosphere surrounding the
case with a treatment plan that includes nursing care, home
management, and minimal goals for the retardate.

This case is cited not to disprove the thesis that individual-
centered versus group-centered orientations provide the major
underlying bases for disagreement, but rather to demonstrate the
difficulty of filtering out any one element as causative. Even if
we proceed on the assumption that the Wellin thesis is substantially true, we still must point out (as he does) that ". . . no
staff member adhered solely to one or the other orientation . . ."[13]
These perfectly natural human inconsistencies tend to mask the
fact that professional orientation serves to create differences in
perceiving a problem. To refer again to the case of the "I" family, the treatment plan "agreed" upon never indicated real con-

---

[13] Wellin, *op. cit.*, p. 6.

sensus. The clinic study director,[14] in discussing the case with the writer, said that he felt the effectiveness of the CSRC was certainly lessened because of the lack of consensus regarding etiology, for it meant that subsequently the treatment plan suffered.

To illustrate what happens in a case like this, let us examine the mother's report of the services she felt helped alleviate the problem. Mrs. "I" reported that the most helpful services were the medical service and the nursery school; in regard to herself, "someone to talk to" and specifically the public health nurse who also helped her with the home management of the retardate.

Case work was not rendered or attempted because the case worker did not agree with the diagnosis of emotional involvement nor that the mother could benefit from such work. Later on, the staff reconsidered the needs of the mother and the retardate, but since the relationship with the nurse had been established, and for other reasons, the treatment plan was not changed.

The second factor affecting consensus, other than professional orientation, is related to the personal equation of interest or lack of interest in a particular family. Here the group worker would recognize at once the problem of group dynamics inherent in the "team" concept. How do you get people to work together? This is a problem of emotions, status, interest, motivation, and other similar factors. A staff member could well decide against working with a family on the basis that (a) someone else can do the job; (b) someone else is better suited to handle the problem; (c) this case doesn't really concern me (doesn't fall within my professional discipline), and (d) this family cannot benefit from my services (case work, speech therapy, or whatever). These judgments, we may note, might be valid, or they might also be rationalizations for not wanting to get involved. The administrator has the difficult task of deciding when judgments are valid, based on professional knowledge, and when they can be correctly labeled as mere rationalizations.

Another element in the personal equation that affects group

---

[14] Simon Olshansky.

decisions is what some writers have labeled "apparent consensus"[15] and others have called "pseudoconsensus." Staff members want to be "liked" and not be regarded as always opposing one or more other staff members. This may, and often does, result in acquiescence regarding a plan of action for which the individual staff member has little interest or personal motivation. The decision was "generally agreed upon." No one person's name is attached to it—hence any failure or criticism of the plan will not be "personal" for any staff member.

The case of the "R" family illustrates these factors which are in addition to or outside of the professional orientation. The "R" family is a multiple-problem family. The index problem was the retardate, but the staff was in agreement regarding the needs of the entire family. Case worker "A" concurred and did an excellent job of working with the family. However, case worker "A" left the agency and incoming case worker "B" did not have the same motivations to work with the "R" family. The insight or perception of these two workers differed so much that no extensive case work was carried on with the "R" family after the departure of case worker "A". When questioned or pushed regarding the lack of work with the family, case worker "B" retreated into giving reasons why the family could not profit from the work. This case may be idiosyncratic in some respects, but the fact remains that such cases do exist and fall outside of the pattern of differences due only to professional orientation.

The third factor affecting consensus is the tendency of some staff members to be rigid regarding a given treatment plan. If giving up an agreed-upon position carries with it an overtone of criticism for the staff member strongly supporting that position, then you have elements making for lack of consensus. A staff member with his own insecurities may insist that his position is "right," and then tend to defend it vigorously to the possible detriment of the treatment plan itself. The previous illustration of Mrs. "I" was also an example of staff rigidity affecting the

---

[15] William Caudill and Bertram H. Roberts: Pitfalls in the organization of interdisciplinary research. *Human Organization Research*, (ed.) Richard N. Adams and Jack J. Preiss, Homewood, Illinois, The Dorsey Press, Inc., 1960, p. 14.

possible revision of a treatment plan. Staff members "A" and "B" were in disagreement regarding the diagnosis of the mother's problem. The case conference represented a compromise with no real agreement. Staff member "B" who should have established a working relationship with the mother felt unable to do so because of her disagreement; therefore, staff member "C" became involved because of prior contacts and did establish a fruitful relationship. "B" never went back to the case and, although the mother's problem was subsequently discussed in case conference, the treatment plan was not changed and worker "B" held rigidly to her previous viewpoint. The services that were undoubtedly needed by the mother therefore were never rendered completely since "C" had to perform not only her own function but also that of "B".

The fourth factor is in some ways related to professional orientation, namely bias.[16] The professional orientation may be conceived of as being an overall or global viewpoint of a particular discipline. A bias within that orientation may be thought of as presenting a certain pattern or line of behavior. An example of bias is the tendency of some members of the team (public health nurse, physician, or speech therapist) to think in terms of the *tangible* aspects of a case (home care, management, removal of physical problems, glasses, etc.). In contrast, bias of the psychologist, social worker, psychiatrist, or nursery school teacher is apt to stress the *intangibles* (the mental health of the parents and siblings, the attitude of the teacher or neighbor towards the retardate, the home environment in respect to attitudes, or consideration, etc.). These biases then tend to emphasize needs which conform to them, and can on occasion result in lack of consensus on what is an important need for a retardate or his family. Fortunately, the team work concept usually results in doing as many different things as possible for the family—action that we may attribute to the variety of disciplines involved—hence, bias does not necessarily work to the detriment of the client.

----

[16] Bias may be favorable or unfavorable and should not be understood as implying prejudice which is usually an unfavorable opinion towards something. Bias in the above connection is regarded as representing a line or direction which is normally pursued.

SUMMARY

The problem of consensus then, under the team concept employed by the CSRC and similar clinics, may hinge on the apparent dichotomy present in the professional orientations toward the "individual" or "group." Professionals of varying disciplines must learn each others' concepts in order to move forward efficiently as a team.[17] The analogy of a concert orchestra is not too far-fetched except that in the case of a concert the music is written out and each member understands his role. The conductor, however, has to bind them all together and utilize to best advantage what each instrument can offer to the whole. A similar situation exists for the director of a clinic who must attempt to bring harmony into the entire clinic program.

In addition to the overall problem related to professional orientations, we have noted four other factors which also influence consensus: (a) lack of etiological clarity; (b) lack of interest or other personal elements; (c) tendency towards rigidity and consequent lack of flexibility regarding treatment plans, and (d) bias.

Awareness on the part of the staff and administrator that these problems are inherent in the team approach will do much to reduce disillusionment, and will improve staff morale. Realization that the above patterns exist elsewhere and with other staffs may result in reducing tension. A staff that can look at itself objectively (and perhaps laugh at some of its dearly-loved concepts) will probably be more effective than the "tight" defensive staff in which each member jealously guards his or her font of wisdom.

Finally, the need for mature, secure staff people is so obvious that it hardly bears repeating. In the field of mental retardation, however, with all of its heartaches for the parents, we cannot afford to accept anything but the very best staff if we are to lighten in every possible way the burden that must be carried.

---

[17] In the context of interdisciplinary research, Caudill and Roberts say, "The extent to which each collaborator comprehends and accepts the basic theoretical formulations of the other's discipline forms the common denominator of the project." Caudill and Roberts, *op. cit.*, p. 14.

Mature, secure professionals sincerely concerned with the child and his family who will operate in the give and take atmosphere of the team approach are the kind of people the agencies need. Their egos should have had sufficient time to mature, and status should be one of their lesser concerns.

Chapter VI

SUMMARY, FINDINGS, AND CONCLUSIONS

THE RESULTS OF this study were helpful in answering to some limited degree questions regarding case finding, how mothers seek services, what mothers think of services rendered, and what kinds of services clinics need to consider Recent dramatic results in cases of phenylketonuria and galactosemia, and the past history of the control of syphilis point up the value of early knowledge and treatment. Next to early case finding, we would place in importance to the retardate and the clinic giving services some knowledge regarding how mothers seek and use treatment and services. This study has helped outline several of the important steps mothers take. Finally, clinical directors may find some of the mothers' opinions regarding services helpful in future planning. These opinions may be faulty as viewed by the clinic, but they represent "reality" to the mothers. Truth in this case may rest more on how the mother views the services and her needs, and not so much on whether or not she is right in her judgment. A clinic for example, may do well to publicize the fact that it has a nursery school as a part of its program even though in the treatment plan for many children the nursery may not play a large part.

FINDINGS

The study resulted in the following twelve findings:

(a) There was evidence that families of working-class and lower-middle-class groups *will* and *do utilize* a publicly supported community service for the evaluation and treatment of their mentally retarded children. No evidence regarding upper-middle-class and upper-class groups was available, but there is a strong suspicion that these groups use medical services only, or make their own decisions regarding private schools or private care and do not come to publicly-supported clinics.

(b) The size of the family seemed not to be a factor in the seeking or not seeking of services for the retarded child.

(c) The average number of children in the families of the sample was 3.7, which compares favorably with the Myerson study of families that had children at the Walter E. Fernald State School or the Wrentham State School in Massachusetts.[1] The families cannot, therefore, be classified as substantially larger than the average for the state.

(d) Consistent with their philosophy of "taking things as they come," the lower-class and lower-middle-class families tended to keep their mentally retarded children in the home as long as possible. Only very severe cases, for example, a very low grade Mongoloid boy of nine who could not learn to control evacuation; and a girl with brain damage and aggravated hyper-activity who could not speak at all, were seen as needing to be institutionalized. In every case where the mothers spoke of institutionalization at all, it was in such severe cases. Parents (at least of the economic and cultural level studied) were consistent in their desire not to "put him away" (in an institution). The expression "to put him (or her) away" seemed to be accompanied usually by the feeling that this was, "of course," not the "right thing to do."

(e) The mothers' education, religion, or ethnic background did not account for any significant differences in the kinds of services they asked for or utilized.

(f) The working-class and lower-middle-class mothers were very willing to talk about their mentally retarded children. Not

---

[1] Stanley Powell Davies, *op. cit.*, p. 90. Davies reports that Myerson's figures were 3.8 for Fernald and 4.5 for the Wrentham School. The Wrentham figure was slightly larger than that for the general population of Massachusetts but no larger than that of the cultural level from which the patients came. Davies also reports on a study by Dr. Neil A. Dayton where the number of children born to native white mothers in the state of Massachusetts having a mentally defective child was 3.3.

one family refused to be interviewed and every mother gave at least the appearance of genuine interest and willingness to answer questions and to talk about whatever would be of help for her and her child. Contrary to the prevalent assumption that lower-class mothers find difficulty in verbalizing, this proved not to be the case. It should be noted that with the exception of one family, all expressed a satisfactory or more than satisfactory experience with the CSRC.

(g) The families in the sample almost without exception did not discuss their needs or problems regarding their mentally retarded children with a priest or minister, although 79 per cent of the sample was of the Roman Catholic faith and although the majority attended mass regularly. There did not seem any indication that these mothers (either Catholic or Protestant) regarded the church as a place to go for help in dealing with their retarded children.

(h) Families with moderately and severely retarded children sought and received services for them usually before they were two years of age.[2] Although the number of cases in the sample was too small to generalize, the childen in the lower-lower-working class received medical services at an average of 12.2 months of age;[3] of the upper-lower-class, at 24.6 months of age, and of the lower-middle-class group, at 22.1 months of age. The only family in the upper-middle-class did not arrive in this country until the retardate was thirty-six months of age.

(i) *Diagnostic evaluation*: Fifteen of the twenty-four mothers coming to the CSRC asked for consultation services, that is, diagnostic evaluation. For the most part they did not know what to expect from the CSRC. They had been referred to it by their private physicians or by members of the medical or social work staff at the Children's Medical Center. All expected to get some

---

[2] The relative newness of the services (the CSRC opened in July, 1957, with the first case in October, 1957) precludes analysis of when children first got to the CSRC. Twenty-three children in the sample studied had already been to other services prior to the above opening date.

[3] This seems to be related to the fact that these mothers received a good deal of free medical service through the well-baby clinics and the public health nurses.

kind of help, but most were not clear about what kind it would be. Although diagnostic evaluation is basic to the kind of treatment prescribed, only fifteen out of the twenty-four mothers, as indicated, came specifically asking for it. As discussed in Chapter V, there is a strong possibility that the mothers really came for some physical service (e.g., Nursery school, or speech therapy). The fact that they asked for consultation service does not necessarily mean that they equated this with diagnostic evaluation until some later date, in which case, what we are really dealing with is a "learned" experience. Parents learn fast the acceptable terminology of the professionals. In the majority of the cases, the mother usually also admitted (although sometimes only after a probe) that having the child at nursery school was a "great relief" to her. Some said it gave them "time to do the housework," or " breather," or "a chance to get the marketing done." Although it was impossible to pinpoint, the interviewer sometimes sensed that the mothers felt guilty about wanting the child out of the home. But this does not minimize the fact that both the children and the mother received some very real help from the nursery school. An example of a typical reaction is Mrs. L, who said that the nursery school helped her "a great deal." She also said,

> My son has learned to do some painting and this now occupies his attention. He has learned to dress himself and he did not know how to do this before. Perhaps it was because I was too ready to help him; but the nursery school teacher has the patience and has taught him how to put on his things and seems to be patient with him even if he does it incorrectly or has difficulty with it.

This mother also had some very strong feelings about the help that she has received from the CSRC and the nursery school which can be stated in her own words: "I would have really been ready for the asylum if it hadn't been for the CSRC and the nursery school."

(j) *Home training service.* This service rendered by the public health nurse was not a service that the mothers "asked for," but almost without exception it was the first service mentioned when the mother was asked, "What helps?" The home visits were perceived as friendly visits, yet "professional," and concerned with the health and welfare of the retarded child. Significantly, mothers used this service to get help for other members of the family and also for neighbors who had children suspected of being slow or retarded. Since CSRC was set up to work with the whole family, the public health nurse saw her role as one of concern for every member of the family. Consequently, as she visited the homes and established a warm and friendly relationship, she was used by the families as a kind of referral service for other members of the family as well. Frequently, the public health nurse was able to spot health or emotional difficulties and refer persons either to the CSRC or other sources in the community for help.

(k) *Extended family and "association of parents" as a help to parents.* Although the findings are limited, due to the small size of the sample, there seemed to be indications that the five mothers who mentioned extended kin relations as "helpful" did in fact receive physical help (e.g., baby-sitting) and perhaps some emotional release. This finding cannot be documented statistically, but the general tone of the mothers in reporting this information seemed to make it obvious that having one's parents or in-laws or other relatives living in the same house or nearby was helpful, especially in those cases where friendly relations existed. A similar observation is reported in Reuben Hill's work about families suffering under the stress of having the father leave for the military service.[4]

Not all mothers, however, were successful in their kin relationships. Each of two mothers, for example, reported that she didn't "have anything to do with my relatives." Further conversation brought out the fact that the relatives "look down on them" (because of economic reasons or because the relatives couldn't face a family with a retarded child). It was obvious that the mothers felt discriminated against because their relatives "thought they were better than we are."

The idea of an "association of parents" is combined with the

---

[4] Reuben Hill, *Families Under Stress*, New York, Harper and Brothers, 1949.

extended family finding because there seems to be an apparent linking of the two ideas. Mothers frequently expressed the need for getting together with other parents who also had retarded children.[5] "Misery loves company," "It's good to talk with others who have the same troubles," "It makes you feel that you aren't the only one in the world who has a retarded child," "People that have a child like this understand what you are up against— others don't." Expressions such as these indicate the latent desire and need to get together with other parents.

The fact is, however, that only three out of the twenty-four mothers actually sought and attended a meeting of the local association for retarded children, although many more expressed an interest in doing so. Questions that need to be answered: (a) Will mothers of lower class or lower-middle class actually attend formal meetings of parents? and (b) If lower-middle and lower classes do not attend formal meetings or seek "associations of parents" what are the reasons? Observation leads to the belief that the persons most often in attendance at meetings of parents tend to be on the upper levels of the middle class (middle and upper-middle). Significantly, upper-class persons are also rarely in attendance.

If associations of parents are important (as we assume they are) because of the emotional release possible through meeting with others, then we need to ask the question: "Do we need to restructure associations and programs so as to enable all class groups to benefit—or shall we knowingly and purposefully leave out the working-class groups?" Although this is not the place to discuss possible program forms, what the writer has in mind is the possibility of informal meetings, small group sessions, "kaffee klatch" affairs, and similar type programs.

CONCLUSIONS

Referring back to the original focus of this inquiry, we had three areas under investigation: (a) early perceptions of the

---

[5] Other writers have pointed to similar findings: Charlotte H. Waskowitz, The parents of retarded children speak for themselves. *J Pediat*, 54:319, 1959; and see also: Joseph Wortis: Mental retardation as a public health problem. *Amer J Public Health*, No. 5, 45:632-636, May 1955.

mothers—when they first surmised or had a suspicion that their children might not be normal;(b) the steps taken by the mothers to seek and use community resources (medical or otherwise), and (c) their reactions toward the services rendered by the community agency (in this case, the CSRC). From the data of the twenty-four interviews in the sample under analysis, the following conclusion may be drawn.

Early perceptions of the mothers, when they first surmised or had a suspicion that their child might not be normal:

(a) In respect to the severely mentally retarded child, the mother recognizes the atypical condition or behavior of the mentally retarded child, but in most cases relates it to a physical rather than a mental condition.

(b) The mothers typically report "being shocked" and "disbelieving when first advised of the mental retardation.

(c) The mothers typically say that they would appreciate being told early and with understanding and compassion, not brutally or thoughtlessly.

The steps taken by the mother to seek and use community resources, medical or otherwise:

(a) The mothers typically did not seem to depend on advice from neighbors, friends, relatives, priests, or ministers, regarding their mentally retarded children. The average mother may have discussed the symptoms with a neighbor or relative, but made an early decision to seek medical help. This finding is all the more interesting because the sample under study is of low and middle economic groups. We may surmise that there are several factors in the Cambridge community that account for this:[6] (1) It is a relatively enlightened community from the health standpoint; (2) the Cambridge Health Department is aggressive; (3) the public health nurses are in attendance in every public and parochial school; (4) articles on health are frequent in the Cambridge and Boston newspapers, and (5) many excellent medical resources in the Boston area are readily available.

(b) As might be expected from a sample of mothers using services of a community agency, they represented a group that

---

[6] These assumptions might well be tested at a later date in a study of the psychosocial dynamics of decision making.

on the whole followed through on the recommendations of the physician or nurse to seek services for their retarded child. However, since no significant numbers of mothers was located outside of this pattern, we may assume that for the class group in this study they do follow through and utilize community agency services.

The reactions toward the services rendered by a community agency:

(a) The mothers were almost without exception very appreciative and satisfied with the kind and variety of services rendered by the CSRC. In response to the question "What kind of service would you add or like to see added?" the mothers could think of no major additions. There were, however, some minor criticisms existing in reference to transportation to the nursery school, and some five mothers voiced their desire that the nursery school be kept open longer. Some also expressed an interest in a day-care program where the children would be taken care of for more hours during the day. Many of these mothers felt that they could cope with the child and keep him at home if they weren't burdened with him twenty-four hours a day. Two mothers criticized "speech therapy" as not being given often enough to be helpful, although other mothers reported that they were "very well satisfied."

(b) Although most mothers said they were satisfied, this should not be interpreted to mean that the program was in reality meeting all the needs. The criticisms were mild, possibly in part because the mothers did appreciate the services rendered and did not want to appear ungrateful. However, some mothers and one father wanted, in addition to day care, a day camp program in the summer. One family moved from Cambridge to a nearby city that offered this type program for mentally retarded children. Supervised recreation was another thing that appealed to some parents, especially those that had seen such a program in operation.

These hints from the parents might well serve to stimulate thinking on the part of those interested in clinics such as the CSRC. The fact that no one really knows the answer to "what is a complete program" means that assuming the role of learner should not be too traumatic. Much more experimentation is apparently necessary with longer hours for nursery schools, day-care programs (and, perhaps in some cases, night-care programs for exhausted mothers who have been awake night after night with children unable to tolerate or utilize tranquilizers), summer day camps, supervised recreation, and perhaps many other "inventions" to help the mothers as well as the retarded children.

Chapter VII

IMPLICATIONS

I MPLICATIONS RESULTING FROM this study will be useful to a variety of groups: (a) professionals who work with retardates and their mothers; (b) parents and parents' associations, and (c) planners, either on the private or public level, who have to make decisions regarding policy, facilities, or programs. Involved in these implication are the role and function of the following: (a) the case worker; (b) the public health nurse; (c) the physician; (d) associations of parents; (e) the clergy; (f) foster home personnel; (g) clinics serving the mentally retarded, and (h) government agencies.[1]

IMPLICATIONS FOR THE CASE WORKER

The major facts of interest to the case worker are that (a) the client very often rejects social work and the case worker, and (b) the case work role often is defined differently by each group—the clients, the various staff members, and the case worker. The rejection of the social worker in a clinical setting in favor of the nurse is a pattern that calls for further examination.[2] Others have

---

[1] This study was completed prior to the great surge forward which took place as a result of the President's Panel on Mental Retardation appointed by President Kennedy on October 17, 1961, with Leonard W. Mayo as chairman. The implications for government agencies resulting from the President's Panel are, of course, far ranging and the most comprehensive the country has yet had in the field of retardation. These implications will be discussed in Chapter IX of the present volume.

[2] This pattern was studied intensively and evaluated by Eliot Friedson, *op. cit.* He reports among his observations that only in regard to ". . . a clearly interpersonal problem" did the social worker displace the nurse as the person to whom the people would turn for advice.

noticed this tendency and attempted new approaches.[3] Considering the very real need for the best possible social services in the mental retardation field, the results of these services seem meager. The importance of adequate and complete services has been spelled out by various writers.[4] The question that needs answering is "What specific and what general functions are expected of the social worker?"[5] Sometimes it was noted in the case conference or in talks with the staff that the case work role was being defined in terms of "counseling," sometimes in terms of "casework."[6] In contrast, the mothers defined the function of the social worker in terms of "asking questions, getting your background, and things like that . . ." (Since the clinic is not a fee charging agency, there was no reference to finances.) Only

---

[3] Helen Beck discusses "cooperative effort" between the public health nurse and the social worker as an "experiment" being carried out at the Mental Retardation Unit, St. Christopher's Hospital for Children, Philadelphia, *op. cit.* See also an excellent detailed description of the case worker's role in the clinic setting, William R. Vath, *op. cit.*

[4] Michael J. Begab has written extensively in this area. See, for example, "Some Basic Considerations in Casework with Mentally Retarded Children and Their Families," U. S. Dept. of Health, Education, and Welfare (mimeographed copy, no date); Child-welfare service for the mentally retarded. *Children,* May-June, 1958; Unmet needs of the mentally retarded in the community. *Amer J Men Defic,* No. 4, Vol. 62, January, 1958. See also Helen L. Beck, *op. cit.,* Howard R. Kelman: Individualizing the social integration of the mentally retarded child. *Amer J Men Defic,* No. 4, Vol. 60, April, 1956; and Rudolph P. Hormuth, *op. cit.*

[5] The term social worker was usually used by the clients, while the clinic staff usually referred to this person as "the case worker." The terms therefore are being used interchangeably in this discussion.

[6] Aptekar defines counseling as helping through discussions with clients around interpersonal problems of living, and case work as offering concrete social services of help to the individual. He points out, too, that although the two terms are very often used synonymously, in his estimation it is important to make a distinction. See Herbert H. Aptekar: *The Dynamics of Casework and Counseling.* New York, Houghton Mifflin Company, 1955.

Helen Beck, Chief Psychiatric Social Worker at St. Christopher's Hospital for Children, Philadelphia, has said that "parent counseling" is descriptive of a "process of case work treatment." See Beck, *op. cit.*

The writer's observation was that at least in the CSRC the staff thought of case work as more related to the Aptekar definition of services, and counseling as more related to "talking to or with the client." As far as the writer knows, no attempt was made to clarify the various functions of the social worker in line with existing concepts.

in a few instances, where mothers had had a satisfactory case worker relationship, was the role defined as "helpful". . . "someone to talk to that understood your problem." Yet, this latter response ought to have permeated the entire sample in terms of the professional expectation of the social worker. All this raises the very real question of whether the job expected of the social worker *in the clinical setting,* and specifically with mentally retarded children, can be satisfactorily performed in an office. The kind of relationship that has to be established on the basis of personal contact, of observation in the home of the retardate, and of personal knowledge of the mother's problems requires a more intimate knowledge than can be derived through an office interview.[7] The various factors discussed indicate some of the problems inherent in the implications for the social work profession. A closer and more detailed examination seems indicated for the future role of the case worker in the clinical team.

IMPLICATIONS FOR THE PUBLIC HEALTH NURSE

From talking with the mothers one gets an image of the public health nurse that is warm, friendly, helpful, and *nonthreatening.* The nurse is welcomed into the home because of her "obvious" helping role, which role is an accepted part of the value organization and cultural pattern of our society. In other words, her place is "structured into society" in such a way that the mother can say (as a number of them did) without any sense of guilt or inadequacy, "The nurse is helping us with toilet-training. We certainly do appreciate all the help she has given us." The mothers feel they can talk to the nurse—and also that she can be an "intermediary" between them and the doctor.[8] This function of the nurse is important to the mothers.

Implied, therefore, in this observation of the role of the nurse is that there is a function of the nurse as "listener" which overlaps

---

[7] See work of Norman Bell, Albert Trieschman, and Ezra Vogel regarding relationship problems with lower working class fathers.

[8] This observation was made also by Ozzie G. Simmons in another cultural setting. See The clinical team in a Chilean Health Center. *Health, Culture, and Community,* (ed) Benjamin D. Paul, New York, Russell Sage Foundation, 1955, pp. 338-339.

the "counselor" role of the social worker (the overlapping areas of competence include other functions as well[9]); and the nurse, because of her acceptable image in the culture (nonthreatening, warm, helpful), is in a position to be of service to the clients. Public health nursing education courses include instruction which overlaps in content the material taught to social workers. The nursing profession is aware of the problem of overlapping areas of competence. The implication may very well be that the other members of the team also need a course of instruction in each of the other disciplines so that a common language and approach may make their work more effective.

IMPLICATIONS FOR THE PHYSICIAN

Time and again the mothers mentioned wanting to hear about their child in a sympathetic and compassionate manner. Apparently there is much that needs to be learned about how to talk to and with parents about their retarded children. As one mother phrased it, "We don't hide them in closets anymore. We realize that anyone can have a retarded child. It isn't that we have the feelings of guilt or shame that so many people used to have, but still it's hard to take (being told your child is retarded) and you want someone to do it in a kind and sympathetic way, as if he really knew what it meant to have a child like this." In discussing the parents' reactions on first learning the diagnosis of retardation, Zwerling says, ". . . appropriate handling by the physician can turn a potentially devastating experience into the foundation for a satisfactory adjustment to the problem and to

----

[9] Gertrude Johnson considers four of the "skills and attributes" of the public health nurse as (a) security in working in the home situation; (b) knowledge of resources which can be utilized for nonnursing problems; (c) basic knowledge of normal child growth and development and (d) the general acceptance by the public of the role and function of the public health nurse. See Gertrude Johnson: The public health nurse and the mentally retarded child. *Public Health News,* New Jersey State Department of Health, September, 1960, p. 324.

In the above article and in others that are published in the nursing journals, one is reminded time and again that the public health nurse particularly is aware and must be aware of cultural differences and influences on attitudes and values. In her home visits she may find it extremely difficult to separate the emotional problems from the "just physical." These two types of problems then are similar to the ones traditionally handled by the social worker.

the child."[10] How the parents are told certainly seems quite as important as what they are told.[11] In the clinic setting, the physician is not always the person who tells the parents; often the social worker handles this delicate assignment. In almost all of the cases in our sample, however, the parents had heard the diagnosis *before* coming to the CSRC and in almost every case it came from a physician—quite often, the pediatrician. Going to the CSRC was more in the nature of asking for a confirmation of the diagnosis and a seeking of services. However, there is a definite implication for the physicians in the mother's reporting a need for an understanding and understandable manner of communicating the diagnosis and prognosis. (We can't assume, for example, that the doctor's statement, "Your child is Mongoloid," really communicates the idea of mental retardation to the mother—as a number of our cases show.) More education along this line for general practitioners, pediatricians, and obstetricians would be one way of getting across this message. Some associations of parents have made up kits of materials which they send to public health nurses, ministers, and others. Some such idea for physicians, coupled with lectures, seminars, and pamphlets to be distributed throughout the community would meet a real need.

IMPLICATIONS FOR THE ASSOCIATION OF PARENTS

During the interviews the mothers frequently mentioned "wanted to attend" meetings with other parents. One mother said, "I know this sounds funny, but somehow you feel better when you see that you're not the only one in the same boat." However, not enough leadership developed in the Cambridge area on its own to form a parents' group. The Boston Association for Retarded Children made several attempts to bring together such a group, but lacking sufficient staff could not spend the time needed to organize the parents. In spite of this seeming contradiction, the parents *wanting* groups and yet not developing

---

[10] Israel Zwerling, *op. cit.*

[11] For a very sensitive and understanding development of this theme see Carl Drayer and Elfriede G. Schlesinger: The Informing Interview. *Amer J Ment Defic*, LXV, No. 3, 65:363-370, November, 1960.

them on their own, it still would appear that the parents feel there is an implied need for such groups. A very serious question needs to be raised, however, as to whether or not lower-class families would join (or attempt to organize) parents' groups of the type currently found throughout the country. For the most part the parents of such groups tend to belong to the middle class with a scattering of upper-middle.[12] It is probable, however, that lower- as well as middle-class persons can be interested and derive benefit from some of the assumed positive values of parents' groups: (a) education regarding problems of their children; (b) release of tensions from talking with other parents; (c) emotional support; (d) outlet for energies, anxiety, frustration, and (d) channeling of efforts into constructive enterprises including lobbying for better or increased services for the retarded.

Negative values may also be postulated: a possible over-emphasis on the handicap and a consequent distortion of a view towards life; disturbed parents may tend to reinforce other disturbed parents. Even though they attempt to get "correct" information, groups with inadequate leadership may well inadvertently disseminate misinformation, and some parents may use such a group to avoid facing their own problems.[13]

Since mental retardation is no respecter of persons, parents' groups need to cover all classes of persons if the assumed values are to be distributed among all parents having such children. There would seem, then, a definite implication for associations of parents and the professionals associated with such groups to give time and thought to an analysis of the group structure with particular attention to the functions served by such groups. A sociological analysis of group structure and role might formulate

---

[12] This impression was gained from observation after attending a number of meetings around the Boston area, and from talking with professionals about groups elsewhere. Unfortunately a recent study by Alfred H. Katz: *Parents of the Handicapped*, Springfield, Charles C Thomas, 1961, does not discuss the self-organized parents' groups in terms of social class. In other respects, however, Katz does describe how these groups come to be organized.

[13] For a more complete discussion of the positive and negative elements, see Joseph H. Levy: A study of Parent Groups for Handicapped Children. *Exceptional Children*, No. 1, Vol. 19, October, 1952; and Helen L. Beck, *op. cit.*

questions such as: Who joins and why? What purposes are served by this structure? What interaction of participants is possible and to what ends? What goals are feasible, reachable, desirable? How are the goals to be achieved? To what degree can parents' groups achieve "success" and in what directions? The answers to these and other questions and the analysis required offer possible help to what appears a growing and necessary movement.

To bring the subject of parents' groups up-to-date, it is important to note that in order to broaden the outlook and bring in a professional viewpoint, the National Association for Retarded Children is encouraging teachers, doctors, lawyers, clergymen, social workers and other professionals, whether they are parents of retarded children or not, to join and participate in state and local chapters.

IMPLICATIONS FOR THE CLERGY

The lack of interest displayed by the mothers included in this study toward talking over their problems with the clergy suggests that perhaps the latter are not sufficiently aware of retardation and its meaning for a family.

In cases of mental illness, the clergy are often consulted by those with mental or emotional problems prior to going to a psychiatrist.[14] Parents of the retarded, however, seem to regard their child's problem as a physical one and therefore do not go to the clergy. The one exception being when such children are ready for communion in the Roman Catholic faith, or for possible attendance at a parochial school. Parents do need counseling and comfort, and very often proper referral to a helping resource. Here the clergy could assume an aggressive role. What is needed is a program of indoctrination for clergymen regarding the problems of the retarded, and resources available to help solve those problems. Such a program for public health nurses has been instituted locally with excellent results,[15] and a similar

---

[14] Gerald Gurin, Joseph Veroff, and Sheila Feld: *Americans View Their Mental Health.* New York, Basic Books, Inc., 1960, p. 308.

[15] The Massachusetts Association for Retarded Children and its affiliated

program could easily be developed for the clergy.

IMPLICATIONS FOR FOSTER HOMES

From talks with parents and with staffs of clinics and institutions, the writer gained the impression that certain types of persons make the best parents for the retarded at home, in foster homes, and in institutions. These persons seem to come from the upper end of the blue collar and the lower end of the white collar groups. This assumption grows out of the impression, gained from the above, that the toleration of deviance is greater among the lower classes. The same observation is made by Hollingshead and Redlich in their New Haven study.[16] Although this implication is offered only tentatively, it may provide a valuable clue to administrators and others seeking foster homes and personnel as institutional cottage parents. For this study, concerned as it is with severely and moderately retarded children, the release from institutions of thousands of the mildly retarded would make available more staff and more beds for those who need them badly. The availability of personnel and foster homes of the proper type (as well as the necessary finances) would make possible the release of some mildly retarded to foster home programs, while in other areas speed up the day of eventual return to society and self-supporting status.

IMPLICATIONS FOR THE CLINIC SERVING THE MENTALLY RETARDED

Although the CSRC is supported by public funds and is available to anyone (there is no fee for services), no upper-class and almost no upper-middle-class families took advantage of the services. How the writer tried to locate families which did not reach the CSRC was discussed elsewhere in this report. What kinds of families do not utilize public services? We can only speculate at this point and hypothesize that they are probably from the upper economic group. The mother who said to the

groups is already following such a program with conferences, and educational materials available. Kits have been made available to nurses and conferences stimulated by the MARC and its affiliated groups.

[16] Hollingshead and Redlich, *op. cit.*, pp. 172-173.

interviewer, "I didn't think the CSRC was for people like us. We can afford to take care of our own problems," was probably voicing the opinion of other mothers in this same upper-middle-class economic group. In this statement there may be a suggestion for the clinic to analyze its role in the community and evaluate the services rendered in terms of social class values.

Attention is called also to the specific need for research in an area of sociological anaylsis that examines the clinic as a social system.[17] Such analysis would explore the role and function of the personnel and of the clinic itself. It would examine, for example, interrelationships of staff and patients, the differentiation of roles, role confusion, role complementation, role integration, the communication and decision-making process, stereotypes and their influence, and staff orientations and their effect. The results of such studies could be extremely valuable in setting up efficient clinical programs based on sound functional and structural analyses which would fulfill the intended purpose of serving the mentally retarded of a community. Without such studies it is possible that agencies may establish service patterns and staffing which may not fulfill completely the needs of a community. That this may be so is all the more evident as we realize, from the evidence of a number of studies which have been referred to, that class differences exist and alter interest and acceptance of services. Adequate and ongoing research of the kind indicated above may help prevent much waste in time and personnel.

Finally, there is a need to spell out the duties and functions of the various staff members in terms of role, agency structure, and the team concept. Some of the difficulties seen by the study director at CSRC are traceable to this need. As indicated earlier, however, the total structure and function of the clinic must first be examined since direction will grow out of such analysis, which

---

[17] Morris S. Schwartz, in the work previously cited, reports on social research in a mental hospital which is very much a delimited and small-scale social system. Similar research, however, could be carried on in an out-patient clinic of the type serving the retarded even though it is not a closed system. The greater number of variables would have to be recognized, however, and dealt with adequately.

in turn will influence the role and function of the staff.

Communicating the story of the clinic to the general public, school personnel, clergy, physicians, nurses, social workers, and other professionals would seem to be a necessary part of the work of the clinic. The job of educating the various individuals and groups that have some professional or personal interest in retardation will have to become structured into clinic programs. The actual public information may be a part of the health department program, for example, but nevertheless, specific account should be taken of the need to educate people regarding retardation.

IMPLICATION FOR GOVERNMENTAL AGENCIES CONCERNED WITH MENTAL RETARDATION

In concluding this list of implications, it seems worthwhile and fitting to discuss those for governmental agencies since a number of important functions can be covered only by them. Certainly one implication seems to be that an up-to-date and usable census of the retarded in any community is necessary if an agency is to work efficiently. The writer is well aware that attempts have been made in this direction, but so far unsuccessfully.[18] Ways and means must be explored to make such a census available, useful, and up-to-date. Without going into detail on how this could be accomplished, it should be obvious that the technical means are available and all that is needed is the desire to make such a survey, plus the necessary finances.

With a complete and accurate census, the next question would be, "Knowing the size of the problem and the degree of retardation, what are the component parts of the total problem and how best can they be attacked?" The next step would involve a more global approach than has been possible up to now, necessitating close examination of the total gamut of services, needs, and problems of the retarded, not only here at home, but abroad.

One might speculate, for example, on what it would mean for the welfare of the retarded to have a comprehensive program extending from the date of case finding (which should be at the

---

[18] Stanley Powell Davies, for example, believes a census is necessary but sees it as impractical in terms of time and money, *op. cit.*, pp. 152-153.

earliest possible age) up through and including adulthood. The financial savings alone would make it worthwhile,[19] but the savings in terms of productive lives is vastly more important.

In conclusion, a comprehensive program for the retarded is regarded then as absolutely essential if we are to make any significant advance in care, treatment, and prevention. In order to make such a program effective, ways must be devised to take an accurate census of the target population, and to pay much more attention to behavioral as well as medical research. Research can unlock many areas now tightly locked by superstition or ignorance. Recent research for example has removed the previous misconception that IQ levels are stationary; that Mongoloids must be institutionalized. Instead, we find that patient, well-qualified teachers working in good teaching environments can raise the IQ as much as ten to fifteen points; that parents receiving assistance from community clinics may, by keeping their Mongoloid child at home and through proper training, advance his functioning by many degrees as over against the average advance in many institutional settings. These and many other research findings must be utilized by all persons concerned as quickly as possible and many more research projects planned which will provide answers.

The most important implication for governmental agencies is that one federal agency must direct a well-coordinated approach to the total mental retardation problem. The Department of Health, Education, and Welfare might designate one bureau or division to be responsible for a comprehensive program which should include a much greater involvement with state programs, which in turn would filter down to local health and welfare department programs. This implication seems to come through loud and clear, otherwise we will see a continuation of the confusion resulting from a lack of clear-cut administrative responsibility. Even with the appointment of one bureau or division within the federal government, there will still be fifty

---

[19] If we take only the cost of institutional care for one retardate for his normal span of life, and figure that he will live at least fifty years, the cost would probably be in excess of 100,000 dollars.

different state programs which will differ from each other in minor to major degrees. A strong federal approach leading to supervision, communication, education, cooperation, and research would seem then to be necessary if we are to mount an overall attack on the problems of mental retardation.

Chapter VIII

SIGNIFICANT SERVICES NOW AVAILABLE

W HAT SERVICES ARE MOST important for the mentally retarded? This question is raised again and again as communities struggle to formulate a realistic budget. The pain is not limited to private agencies harassed by too few dollars and too many needs, it is also felt by government agencies who yearly must convince legislators of the worth of their programs. Perhaps all this pain is necessary, if for no other reason than the fact that making clear to others the "whys" and "wherefores" helps to sharpen the agency's concepts of what is most important and where the funds would be most useful.

What services are most important? For those personally or professionally concerned with mental retardation the answer to that question is apt to be, "They are *all* important!" Knowing the value of many varieties of services, parents and professionals react as would a surgeon faced with the question, "If you could afford to take only one instrument into the operating room, which one would it be?" Phrased this way, it is easy to see that setting priorities can become almost a hopeless muddle. All services tend to dovetail. The person needing remedial type education moves from that program to vocational training, to the need for a job, and perhaps counseling in order to find and keep the job. Lacking the counseling component a retardate may be unable to find or keep the job, thereby making valueless the training for which the school or sheltered workshop has spent hundreds or thousands of dollars. Can we say then which services are most important? The answer plainly is not possible in terms of any simple priority listing.

North Carolina is a remarkable example of what a state, until very recently almost devoid of services, can do for the mentally retarded. Governor Sanford, speaking before the White House Conference, told how his state approached the problem of decision-making regarding service needs: "In North Carolina alone we have some 140,000 persons who are classified as mentally retarded. Until very recent years, the best a person afflicted with mental retardation could hope for in my state was custodial care, and much of that was of questionable standards."[1] In 1962, however, the Governor appointed a Commission for the Mentally Retarded and charged them with the obligation of making a thorough study and coming up with recommendations. In 1963, the General Assembly, based on the Commission's report, established a continuing advisory council on mental retardation, financed by the State. This was implementation of one of the recommendations of the President's Panel that each state should make arrangements for planning and coordination of state and local services by establishing an interdepartmental committee, council, or board.[2] It is significant that a state in which the Governor himself recognizes a paucity of services for the retarded could within one year move forward to the establishment of an advisory committee and develop a coordinated approach to meeting the needs.

In addition to the work of coordinating services of the state mental health department, public health, state and local departments of welfare, education, probation, parole and correction, services were quickly developed in North Carolina in eight major categories:

(a) Maternal, preventive, and diagnostic services, largely public health in nature and aimed at prevention.

The Public Health Department developed four child development clinics staffed by pediatricians, psychologists, social

---

[1] The Honorable Terry Sanford: A state program in mental retardation. *The White House Conference on Mental Retardation: Proceedings*, U. S. Department of Health, Education, and Welfare, 1963, p. 31.

[2] The President's Panel on Mental Retardation: *A Proposed Program for National Action to Combat Mental Retardation*, U. S. Government Printing Office, 1962, p. 166.

workers and nurses; five speech and hearing centers, and seven primary centers for premature care. Additional clinics for development evaluation are in progress.

(b) Counseling services now available only to a limited degree at the comprehensive clinics, residential centers, and from public welfare workers are seen as an important service which will be increased as the community mental health clinics and centers come under the Department of Mental Health.

(c) Special classes operating within the public schools were increased from 150 to 553; an additional 100 are planned for 1965.

(d) Vocational training has been given greatly increased funds and emphasis placed on more training units and facilities. Regarding numbers trained, the figure was seven in 1959 and ninety-three in 1962. Although this indicates progress, the state sees much that still needs doing in this field.

(e) "Half-way houses" with provisions for vocational training were set up. This service using rehabilitation counselors emphasizes getting the retarded into some kind of work at the earliest opportunity.

(f) Residential care has grown from a budget of 1.7 million dollars in 1953 to $4.5 million in 1963. The need for training professional staff has been joined with the program by building an in-patient facility for the diagnosis and short-term treatment of mentally retarded and emotionally disturbed children at the state's University Medical Center in Chapel Hill.

(g) Research on learning and retardation is being carried on by various departments at the state university and at the residential centers. Research is regarded as important at all levels—the university, the residential centers and the evaluation clinics—and research projects are in progress in all three.

(h) The State Department of Public Welfare is regarded as pivotal in North Carolina cooperative planning for licensure and supervision of private facilities. The county Departments also play an important role in almost every one of the seven categories previously mentioned. County departments, for example, are particularly interested in diagnostic and treatment services.

Psychologists are employed by the Department of Public Welfare; homemaker services, pioneered early by North Carolina, makes services available to families with retarded, both children and adults.[3]

This quick review of what one state views as significantly needed services is valuable as a way of pointing out that (a) important services may be quickly organized; (b) in most cases we already have in existence or readily available all of the ingredients for the establishment of services, and (c) a firm hand (in this case, the governor's) along with a council or board of knowledgeable and influential citizens can quickly stimulate effective action. Such progress in a short space of time should encourage states which have previously been slow to recognize the large scale needs of the mentally retarded.

COORDINATION AND PLANNING AT THE STATE LEVEL

It is difficult to select any one or more states to serve as models for overall coordination and planning. The North Carolina example described above is well documented by Governor Sanford and is in the White House Conference report previously mentioned. In a booklet, *Report of the Task Force on Coordination,* some fifteen states are listed as "selected examples" and their coordinating and planning programs are described. Uniformity is not reflected in the plans and the possibility that various arrangements may be quite workable is noted. One pattern followed in a number of states is to have an interdepartmental committee composed of state department and state agency heads; other states have such a committee but it is composed of qualified professional and lay people who are not employed by the executive branch, and still other states have put together a hybrid or composite body. The important point is that definite forward movement for greater coordination and planning is fast becoming a reality as more and more states respond to the challenges laid down by the President's Panel in its historic document, *A Proposed Program for National Action to Combat Mental Retardation.*

---

[3] Adapted from Terry Sanford's report previously mentioned.

PROGRAMS OF THE FEDERAL GOVERNMENT

The Department of Health, Education, and Welfare has the primary responsibility within the federal government for all activities relating to mental retardation. There are six operating agencies within the department which administer some portion of the various programs. These agencies are the Public Health Service, the Welfare Administration, the Office of Education, the Social Security Administration, the Vocational Rehabilitation Administration, and the Food and Drug Administration.

Programs administered fall into four broad categories: (a) research and studies of various kinds; (b) grant programs for professional preparation in the field; (c) services, and (d) construction of facilities qualifying under the hospital and medical facilities program.

Research. Activities in the field of research are not all administered by one bureau of the federal government. Significant research programs, for example, are being carried on by the Children's Bureau, the Bureau of State Services, the National Institutes of Health (and by its several component parts: the National Institute of Child Health and Human Development, the National Institute of Neurological Disease and Blindness), and by the Bureau of Educational Research and Development.

Maternal care is receiving special emphasis partly as a result of the recommendations of the President's Panel which again called attention to the very large group of mildly and moderately retarded that come from low income groups. Women in this group tend to have little or no prenatal care and therefore the highest percentage of complications, often resulting in prematurely born and brain damaged children. A provision of Public Law (P.L.) 88-156 authorizes the Children's Bureau to make grants, contracts, or other arrangements for research projects evaluating and improving services to mothers and their children. A sum of up to eight million dollars per year has been allocated for this research.

Research personnel being in short supply is being given special attention through the passage of Public Law (P.L.) 88-164 which allows construction of facilities which may be used for research, training, and services. This latter combination (research, training, and services) is imperative to the advancement of knowledge and the utilization of research findings. Although to date very little has been accomplished, a number of states are pushing forward on this program. For this aspect of university-affiliated facilities the law has authorized appropriations of 32.5 million dollars for the fiscal years 1964 through 1967.

Coordination between special education and vocational rehabilitation agencies and coordination of community resources for the mentally retarded is receiving special attention from the Vocational Rehabilitation Administration. Selected demonstration projects with a research emphasis will examine the need in this area.

Education of the mentally retarded is the special concern of the Division of Handicapped Children and Youth, Office of Education. Research projects are supported which relate directly to improving the educational situations and developing knowledge in this field.

For demonstration projects in diagnostic services, adolescent retardation, and improvement of services in institutions, the Public Health Service will spend approximately seven million dollars during 1965.

Grant Programs for Professional Preparation. Professional preparation programs are supported by the Department of Health, Education, and Welfare in the areas of research, rehabilitative services, and in-service training of workers in institutions. Title III, of P.L. 88-164 also makes funds available for the Office of Education, which has been able to award fellowships and traineeships to over 2,400 persons in training as teachers of the mentally retarded.

Services. The federal government is involved in a great variety of indirect services which at different levels may become direct services. Examples of federal services include demonstration projects, research, and training programs, Children's Bureau programs which make possible clinics in local communities, and similar programs, all of which eventually mean more and better services to the actual retardate. Income payments under public assistance and social security programs are more clearly a direct service to the retarded. Other programs such as grants for training of personnel, enforcement of the food and drug laws, and technical assistance are all vital and significant services even though they are of a more indirect nature.

Construction of Facilities. Three types of facilities are provided for under Title I of P.L. 88-164. Research centers, university affiliated, and community facilities may be constructed with the funds available to this program which is administered by the Public Health Service. The training of research personnel is one aspect already dealt with under research. The research centers are especially focused on the development of new knowledge useable in preventing and combating mental retardation. Community facilities are offering diagnostic treatment, education, and training services.

STATE AND LOCAL RESPONSIBILITIES

Although the federal government's role in mental retardation has only been summarized in the last few pages, it has become obviously a massive attack on the total program. The federal government, however, has planned most of the programs so that the intitiative must still be taken at the state and local levels. Money and expert help is available through the federal government, provided the state does its share in planning and makes a financial contribution in some cases. Local programs also must be stimulated at the grass roots level but can then take advantage of certain federal programs.

An exciting example of national and local cooperation is the recently funded programs developed by the National Association for Retarded Children (NARC) in cooperation with twenty-one local units throughout the country. Ten of the programs have received funds from the U.S. Department of Labor, through the Manpower Development and Training Act (MDTA).[4] In setting up the program, the NARC officials pointed to evidence that 85 per cent of all retarded persons can be entirely or largely self-

---

[4] See Title II, Manpower, Development and Training Act of 1962 (P.L. 87-415).

sufficient. The problem is that although progress has been made by the schools and the vocational employment programs, there is still a wide gap between employment potential and job opportunities offered to the mentally retarded. Five objectives were set up to attempt to remedy the need in this area:

(a) To develop at least twelve demonstration projects to expand employment opportunities for the mentally retarded.

(b) To develop demonstration projects to train subprofessionals to work with the mentally retarded.

(c) To coordinate community resources (private and public agencies, unions, businesses, etc.) in order to develop an on-going plan for job and training possibilities.

(d) To increase the skills of the retarded in order to upgrade jobs.

(e) To coordinate and exchange information with cooperating public and voluntary agencies on demonstration projects for the mentally retarded and feed back this information into the Manpower Development and Training activities.[5]

Occupational objectives sought were in the field of unskilled and semiskilled work. The largest number of trainees were in the service occupations: hospital aides, food-service and retirement-home aides. Other jobs not usually considered for the retarded were key punch operating personnel trained in cooperation with the International Business Machine Corporation, glass engraving, meat cutting and handling operations (this latter program of meat preparation has great possibilities in the fast expanding food packaging industry and has heretofore been closed to the retarded).

Presently there are ten funded programs; two examples may suffice to give the general format:

(a) *The Human Resources Foundation, Albertson, Long Island, New York,* under the NARC contract with Office of Manpower, Automation and Training (OMAT) developed a program for ninety mentally retarded and/or other severely handicapped youths aged sixteen to twenty-five. Training is being given in key punch operation, typing, and glass

---

[5] National Association for Retarded Children: *A National Project to Promote Employment of the Mentally Retarded: Final Report,* December 1964, p. 2.

engraving (the latter using Panograph-Kino mechanism techniques). Trainees are referred by the New York State Employment Service and the local New York Division of Vocational Rehabilitation. Applicants are screened, the DVR provides medical, psychological, and vocational evaluation and personal adjustment training prior to the training program. During the first thirteen weeks trainees receive full-time training allowances, afterward a combination of paid work and training allowances, full time paid work at $1.25 per hour is expected at the end of the year.

(b) *The Retarded Children's Society of Dade County, Miami, Florida,* in a similar contract, developed a program for fifty underemployed or unemployed retarded youths, aged seventeen to twenty-one with IQ's ranging from 65 to 75. This program was developed with the cooperation and approval of the local meat-cutters' union to demonstrate that many educable retarded are capable of being trained to work as meat cutters, meat wrappers and meat handlers in regular retail and wholesale establishments. Referral, initial evaluation, and certification for training is handled by the Florida State Employment Service. The Miami Division of Vocation Rehabilitation provides medical and psychological examinations, helps develop admission criteria, and assists in the screening of applicants.

Although further examples would be redundant, one previously mentioned fact does bear repeating: cooperation with the federal government can and will make possible a great variety of programs at the local level, but only when combined with state agencies all working together on the problem of retardation.

OTHER STATE-FEDERAL OPPORTUNITIES REGARDING EMPLOYMENT OF THE RETARDED

Cooperation with the federal government sometimes involves a number of state agencies that must combine their efforts in order to devise a comprehensive program for the retarded. An example of a complicated arrangement which is working successfully is the experience of the Texas Education Agency, the state agency responsible for the disbursement of funds in Texas. This agency developed a plan for the rehabilitation of the mentally retarded through a cooperative program between the Divisions of Vocational Rehabilitation and Special Education of the Texas Education Agency and the Special Education programs of certain independent school districts of Texas. Funds already committed by the state education divisions were used to comply with the federal regulations of approximately 35 per cent state, 65 per cent federal (the percentages vary from state to state according to the economic index established).

The Texas program is designed to meet the needs of the educable mentally retarded and is developed at eight levels. *Level I, Preprimary,* is for pupils ages six to about nine with mental ages from three and a half to almost five. The work of the school is centered on motor and sensory training, personal hygiene, habit training, and simple tasks having a carry-over in the home and community. *Level II, Primary* (ages nine to eleven, and mental ages five to six). A carefully structured program moves the child forward at his own speed and toward specific goals. *Level III, Intermediate* (ages eleven to thirteen, mental ages six to nine). Formal instruction is begun in basic communication and arithmetic, but social values are also stressed so that the students feel personal progress is being made.

Levels IV and V are junior high school levels and housed on a junior high school campus. *Level IV, Introduction to Vocations* (chronological ages thirteen to fifteen). This important level aims at introducing the student to the world of work opportunities through field trips, films, speakers, instruction in getting along with fellow workers, filling out job applications, and preparing for job interviews. Social relations are considered important and the student is in at least one class with a regular student in music, art, homemaking, physical education or similar classes. *Level V, Exploring Vocations* (chronological ages fourteen to sixteen. This level actually places the student in a work situation within the school or on campus, rotating him from job to job in order to explore various vocational possibilities. These jobs are not remunerative either for the student or the school.

Levels VI and VII are carried on at the high school level, based on a high school campus. *Level VI, On-Job-Training* (students sixteen years of age and older). This level is geared to learning on a job. The student works part time or full time. Vocation adjustment and evaluation are significant parts of the program. The student is aided by the vocational adjustment coordinator (through the Division of Vocational Rehabilitation) and arrangements are made for job training, placement, supervision, and most important, cooperative planning and working with the local special education department. *Level VII, Employment* (students sixteen years of age and older). This level is for those ready to go out and get a job. The student is coached in how to behave so that he can get and keep a job, and what to do when confronted with certain on-the-job problems. At this point, and providing the student has obtained a job, he is given a diploma of graduation which differs in only one respect from the diploma granted any other student in the Texas schools: his is stamped Special Education Program. *Level VIII.* A final postschool level designed so that the vocational rehabilitation counselor will keep in contact with the student for some time after school graduation and until the case is officially closed.

One significant aspect of the Texas plan has already been mentioned—the cooperation of two divisions within the Texas Education Agency with the local independent school districts and with the Federal-State Vocational Rehabilitation program. The second significant aspect is the comprehensive nature of the program which made important provisions for social and job adjustments. This aspect is based on evidence that seems to indicate that the mentally and physically handicapped lose jobs more often by failure to adjust to a work situation than through inability to perform the job. The Texas Education Agency therefore laid stress in their program on supervision, careful initial training through preemployment and employment and lastly through a follow-up after employment. The program has been regarded very highly by officials of a number of other states who have in turn adapted it to their own uses.[6]

------

[6] Information on the Texas Education Agency program was supplied by George B. Clark, Consultant on Vocational Rehabilitation and Employment, National Association for Retarded Children, Inc., formerly with the Texas Education Agency.

UNIVERSITY PROGRAMS

Five years ago one had to look hard to find any significant professional preparation going on at the college or university level which was specifically directed to the field of mental retardation. Newark State College in Union, New Jersey, is an exception to this statement and has been a center for training teachers of the mentally retarded for more than ten years, offering both an undergraduate and graduate sequence in the field of education of the retarded. With this one exception then, most schools presently involved in professional preparation are newcomers to the field.

Programs are being developed currently, however, in a large number of universities. These generally are (a) for the training of various professionals (social workers, teachers, physicians, biologists, nurses and others), and (b) for research into a variety of medical and sociocultural aspects of retardation.

As mentioned earlier, the federal government is playing a larger part in expanding both professional training and research. However, the role of the National Association for Retarded Children ought to be emphasized even though quantitatively it handles smaller sums of money. A top research advisory board has stimulated and supported important programs in professional training and research, which are carried on by university faculty for the most part, although some research foundations, centers, and hospitals are also involved.

THE WORK OF PRIVATE GROUPS

The work of the National Association for Retarded Children has been dealt with in part throughout this chapter. Further mention will be made in the next chapter regarding prospects for the future. A brief summary of this national organization's work with its 976 units, as of 1964, and enrollment of over 100,000 members will reveal a number of significant programs.

Volunteer Leadership Training. Using some funds received from the Joseph P. Kennedy, Jr. Foundation and NARC general funds, a leadership training program for volunteers was instituted in 1963. A series of institutes have been held in various regions of the country, which in turn energized local institutes in Pennsylvania, Connecticut, and New Jersey. The success of all these institutes has made this an ongoing program.

Legislation. Successful passage of P.L. 88-156 (the Maternal and Child Health and Mental Retardation Planning Amendments of 1963) and P.L. 88-164 (Mental Retardation Facilities and Community Mental Health Centers Construction Act of 1963), both measures strongly supported by NARC, has made it possible for NARC to offer important assistance to state governments, state and local parents' association and others, and to utilize the various programs made financially feasible as a result of the new legislation. This significant service to state planning bodies will "pay off" increasingly as both public and private planning groups utilize the consultants and publications of the NARC office.

Research. This has already been mentioned. Suffice it to say that NARC officials and board members are now supporting, and will continue to support as strong a program of research as possible. NARC is convinced that only through research and the application of research findings is it possible to reach the goal of prevention; to develop more effective methods of care, and to understand better the needs of the retarded.

Other Services. In addition to working with the federal government on vocational rehabilitation and other programs, other services are in the area of publications and consulting. To implement all of the work of the association, six regional "community service" offices have been established. This expansion of the national office into six regions means that state and local units will be receiving important services quickly as needs develop.

Many additional services could be listed, but this high-lighting of some of the more significant services will suffice to show the scope of work done by the national association.[7]

State, regional or city wide associations also conduct a wide gamut of services. Obviously, it is impossible to list all of the significant services being performed by hundreds of such groups.

---

[7] From, *1964—A Threshold Year*, NARC Annual Report and personal interview with Luther W. Stringham, Executive Director, NARC.

Two programs, however, have come to the attention of the writer which bear mentioning since they seem to have most of the best features of such associations.

The first is a very comprehensive program now operating in Bridgeport, Connecticut, begun by the Parents and Friends of Mentally Retarded Children of Bridgeport, Inc. In 1951, this group organized public school classes in cooperation with the Bridgeport superintendent of schools. In March, 1956, they organized a diagnostic and evaluation clinic using the volunteer services of a physician-surgeon, a pediatrician, and a psychologist. Presently, the clinic, which has now been named the Kennedy Center (not named after the late president or any member of his family), has a staff consisting of a dentist, a speech therapist, a social worker, a vocational counselor, and a number of medical consultants.

Policies and operation of the Center are established annually by an elected board of directors. A paid director is administratively responsible. The Bridgeport program includes preschool for children ages three or over with public school potential, a day care program for ages three through adulthood to train for self-care and possible entry into other programs at the Center or elsewhere in the community; a vocational training and sheltered workshop program, and speech and play therapy. A craft shop is also maintained for boys able to use woodworking tools.

The Center maintains a social service program with a full time family counselor available to help families with their retarded children. The counselor acts as a bridge between the family, the Center, and the community. A wide spectrum of other services include religious classes, scouting, summer day camp, resident camp, and recreation activities of all sorts.

The Greater Boston Association for Retarded Children, Inc., provides an example of a program while not as comprehensive (it does not for example, include diagnostic and evaluation clinics, since in the Boston area there are a number of such services available,[8] yet covering a broad spectrum. Programs of GBARC

---

[8] Children's Hospital, the Massachusetts General Hospital, the Cambridge Developmental Clinic, and the various state schools all do diagnostic and evaluation workups.

include preschool nursery classes for ages three to six; training classes, both educational and social, for ages sixteen to thirty-five; a vocational adjustment center for ages sixteen to thirty-five; Saturday night parties for ages sixteen to thirty-five; a social group for boys from three communities in one center, for ages eleven to sixteen; Scouting; a Saturday afternoon recreation program and counseling programs for parents.

The education training program of GBARC offers music, home economics, physical education, academic subjects, dancing, and ceramics. Tuition of twenty dollars to thirty dollars is charged and students are issued public transportation tokens. The vocational adjustment center is staffed by the director, rehabilitation coordinator, psychiatrist, psychologist, sociologist, training supervisors for male and female students, and a shop supervisor. Volunteers from surrounding universities are used extensively. The center does subcontract work designed to give a realistic work experience: collating jobs, mailing, limited furniture refinishing, packaging, printing of letterheads, business cards, envelopes, construction of bookcases, and small parts assemblies.

The Boston association has been able to fashion its program to include the existing facilities and services of local community programs. The Children's Hospital and Massachusetts General are two prime examples of top flight diagnostic facilities available. Similarly, GBARC is able to use the local Family Service Agency program for referral purpose and in turn have clients referred to them by the Family Service. State financed nursery schools which make evaluations are also used by GBARC so that their total program reflects a spectrum of services available throughout the community.[9] Throughout the United States, there are great gaps in services and no one private or public agency can cover everything. Wherever there is a possibility of cooperation, however, this ought to be seized upon by the local group. As regional centers and regional programming, such as the Connecticut State programs, become reality, private agencies

---

[9] Information about GBARC from William Perry, Executive Director, Greater Boston Association for Retarded Children.

will be able to gear in their own local programs, thereby making them even more effective.

EVALUATION OF PROGRAMS FOR THE MENTALLY RETARDED

The great variety and extent of public and private services for the retarded which have proliferated during the last five years makes some kind of systematic evaluation of programs a necessity. As the writer stressed at the beginning of this chapter, it is extremely difficult to set up any priority—placing one service as more necessary than another. But, somehow the need to back away occasionally and look at the larger picture is important, as is the answer to the question, "How are we doing—in respect to all of the needs of the retarded?" To do this kind of evaluative job requires a trained research staff with a real commitment to the field of retardation. Federal grants are now available for such evaluative studies (the writer himself was a member of the Manpower Study Task Force of the Massachusetts study group). A series of task forces were set up under this program to look at specific areas of concern: special education provisions; influence of social environment on mental retardation; manpower, and so forth. Representatives from public and private agencies, universities, state departments of public health, mental health, and rehabilitation were represented on the task forces. This type of evaluation program should be seen as significant and one which states will carry on from time to time. Evaluation is a difficult task but ways and means must be found to do the job well, so that only the best programs will be available for the mentally retarded.

Chapter IX

PROSPECTS FOR THE FUTURE
A GROWING PROBLEM

T HE CONTINUING POPULATION growth indicates that in absolute numbers we must prepare for another million retarded by 1970, for a total of 6.4 million unless there are significant breakthroughs resulting from medical or sociological research which reduces the 3 per cent figure used for estimating retardation. The Economic Opportunity Act, as a practical program offering prekindergarten and enriched educational opportunities, may reduce the number of mildly retarded. Whether or not this will amount to any significant numbers depends on a variety of uncertain factors: continued public interest, money, manpower, parents who take advantage of the programs for the education of their children, international and local peace, political concern, and finally the degree of acceptance of various racial groups.

A second factor of concern in planning for the future is the increase in older retardates, many of whom are now surviving their aged parents. Prior to our increased medical knowledge, retardates died very often before reaching twenty years of age. This was especially true of Mongoloids. The control of tuberculosis, diptheria, pneumonia, scarlet fever, and whooping cough, to mention just a few diseases previously capable of reducing the highly vulnerable retarded population, has begun to be reflected in an ever increasing older population of retarded.

A third factor imbedded in this growing problem relates to the mildly retarded or those on the fringes of retardation who are presently, and will be increasingly, affected by the developments

116

of automation. The new technologies are especially hard on those with limited education who end up in nonskilled or marginally skilled employment. Here the inability to adjust to or absorb academic subject material results in assignment of the worker to a low status, low pay job. Psychologically, this factor alone may be quite a burden for an unskilled person; the problem is increased many times over when, through no fault of his, even the simple job he had is dispensed with through the use of automated equipment. In the large cities the increasing use of automatic elevators is one small example of replacing unskilled people through automation.

Although it is not possible to estimate with any degree of accuracy the number of retarded apt to show up in the ranks of the marginally skilled and unskilled workers laid off because of automation, there is every indication that this can be a large group. Public welfare departments in most cases cannot obtain clinically valid diagnoses of retardation in their clients, yet officials tend to agree that substantial percentages of their case loads are probably mild to moderately retarded. The U. S. Department of Labor programs under the Manpower Development and Training Act (MDTA) have in the initial two years of the program selected less than 3 per cent of their trainees from the group with an education below eighth grade,[1] thus ruling out the great majority of the marginally retarded. It should be noted however that a number of significant demonstration programs are in process under the auspices of the MDTA. (See Chapter VIII.) Regardless, then, of the programs of public welfare, the department of labor, and the Office of Economic Opportunity, the number of retarded unemployed relative to the total unemployed may be expected to increase until specialized training programs are developed for the retarded group. The work of NARC and MDTA in cooperatively setting up demonstration programs as previously cited might be expected to eventually correct this growing trend. Likewise, the development of special programs by public welfare departments and other public and private

---

[1] U. S. Department of Labor: *The Mentally Retarded: Their Special Training Needs,* Manpower Research, Bulletin 6, October, 1964, p. 12.

agencies may also be expected to help correct this trend if the programs become sufficiently large in scope. However, without substantial effort especially directed towards the retarded, we may expect them to show up in ever increasing numbers among the unemployed.

HELP FOR MOTHERS

The importance of the family unit for the growth and development of the retardate in the past has occupied the attention of some researchers,[2] but recently some exciting new developments have encouraged a more careful second look at some of the implications of family life. In the Brooklands experiment conducted in England by Tizard,[3] although directed specifically to an examination of how trainable children would react in a small residential unit, the results indicated that through the use of family type units with parent surrogates, significant improvements resulted in verbal intelligence and speech and motor adjustment. The positive results obtained in this experiment suggest not only that small special purpose residential facilities with surrogate parents are valuable, but contain clues for ways of working with families and particularly with mothers in methods of child development. It has been the observation of the present writer that mothers are anxious to learn how they can help their retarded children. The services of the professional directed to this end might be expected to reduce some of the strain on mothers who daily have to cope with their retarded children.

The report of the President's Panel reminds us that "No mother can be expected to carry the responsibilities of a retarded child without outside support."[4] This help needs to be specified and plans put into operation which will actually offer *direct* services to the mothers. Too often the direct service offered by professional homemaker or the visiting nurse is not available

---

[2] See work by Farber, Angell, Douglass and Children's Bureau.

[3] J. Tizard: "The Residential Care of Mentally Handicapped Children," *Proceedings of the London Conference on the Scientific Study of Mental Deficiency*, 1962, pp. 659-666.

[4] The President's Panel on Mental Retardation: *A Proposed Program for National Action to Combat Mental Retardation*, U. S. Government Printing Office, October, 1962, p. 89.

except in a very few areas. Sometimes these and other much needed direct services are available in one town but unavailable in the very next. To the mother of a retarded child, the reasons for these inequalities make no sense at all. Uniformally direct services then are to be urged for every one of our states. Families now carry the principal burden of caring for the retarded (approximately 96 per cent of the retarded live in the communities, while only 4 per cent are institutionalized). Our concern is how to provide as much help as possible to this large group of parents.

A very direct approach to helping families has been suggested in the Report of The Mission to Denmark and Sweden.[5] In the implications and recommendations section, the mission discusses a philosophical base, administrative structures, programs and services, personnel and research. In programs and services[6] three suggestions are made which are strongly supported by the writer from his experience with mothers of retarded children: (a) the establishment of short-term residential facilities designed to give families or foster families a temporary rest from the routine of caring for their severely retarded child; (b) the extensive use of trained social workers to effectuate successful integration of a variety of services available in the community, and (c) the provision of financial support to assist parents in keeping their retarded child in his own home.

The care of retarded children is so physically wearing on mothers that the establishment of adequate short-term residential facilities would be a tremendous boon. The availability of such facilities would make it possible for the retarded to stay in their own homes and communities and, with additional help to the mother as needed, make possible a level of care which can scarcely be provided by the average institution. True, there are problems which will need researching. No one is suggesting the establishment of short-term residential homes as substitutes for long-term care, or instead of needed community clinics. The effect on the retardate of being even temporarily removed from

---

[5] The President's Panel on Mental Retardation, *Report of the Mission to Denmark and Sweden,* U. S. Department of Health, Education, and Welfare, Public Health Service, 1963, p. 30.

[6] *Ibid.,* pp. 30-32.

his home would need evaluation and study; similarly the effect on the family would need to be assessed. The popularity of the short-term program in Denmark, however, should at least lead us to some demonstration research-action programs in this country.

The second recommendation of the mission report is particularly important to schools of social work. As mentioned earlier in this book, the role of the social worker has not been clearly enough defined (relative to cases of retardation) so that community clinics and out-patient services utilize the services of the social worker to the best advantage. In light of the successful use of social workers in Denmark and Sweden in integrating available services, a prospect for the future in this country suggests study by schools of social work, and demonstration programs to test the amount and kind of social work services needed.

The third recommendation is to consider seriously giving financial support to assist parents. This is such a practical recommendation that any demonstration which can prove its feasibility in this country ought to lead to national legislation at the earliest moment. Again, this recommendation is based on the values inherent in keeping the retardate at home if at all possible. Financially assisting parents so they can pay for homemaker assistance, occasional nursing care, medical supplies, even baby-sitters would possibly make the difference between continuing care at home versus institutionalization. One of the recent task force reports emphasized that

> A most basic element in the therapeutic (including educational) efforts for the retarded patient are his parents, particularly his mother. Whenever the mother has sufficient capacities for understanding and cooperation she should be enlisted as the *major community resource*. The mother usually possesses strong motivation to provide care—a major difficulty in many out-of-home programs.[7]

The various task forces of the President's Panel have recom-

---

[7] U. S. Department of Health, Education, and Welfare, *Report of the Task Force on Prevention, Clinical Services and Residential Care,* August, 1962, p. 36 (see also pp. 36-37).

mended the availability of a continuum of services for the retardate; that these services may well need to be focused on the family of the retardate as well has not yet been spelled out in sufficient detail. The desirability of doing so through studies and demonstrations seems evident.

We are dealing here with prospects for the future; therefore, the emphasis has been on those services and programs which have not yet been instituted or insufficiently exploited; sight must not be lost, however, of the need to improve significantly some of our present services, such as earlier case finding, information and referral, homemakers, nursery and day care, and the whole gamut of community clinical and medical resources necessary for evaluation and treatment.

COMMUNITY SERVICES FOR THE ADULT RETARDED

The growing number of adult retarded will make it necessary to plan a wide spectrum of services for this particular group. Action will be forced upon us by the sheer numbers surviving their parents, the economic waste of thousands of unemployed or underemployed retardates and the cost (not to mention the inhumanity) of just paying retardates to sit out years of life, awaiting death without a job of any significance.

Three categories in which adult retardates need service are (a) personal; (b) employment, and (c) housing. Services, of course, have been available in all three areas but the programs have been spotty, in short supply, and in some geographic areas, nonexistent.

For the future, effort must be concentrated on supplying for the adult retardate, whether in urban or rural areas, a complete spectrum of services.

Personal. Life counseling, available for his entire life span, is basic to a complete service for the retardate. An ongoing consistent counseling program must be available to assist the retardate with his medical, psychological, social, recreational, legal, or other personal problems. *Medically,* the retarded need on-going services since in a great many cases they have physical difficulties along with their retardation. *Psychologically,* the retarded are apt to be subjected to additional stresses of a mental or emotional nature with which the non-retarded are able to cope. *Socially,* the retarded are in need of human interaction as much as normal persons. Parents' associations have realized this for a long time and have consequently developed some excellent programs. Social workers have also become interested recently in the application of group work techniques to the work with retarded.[8] Further investigation into the use of group work and recreational techniques with retarded are necessary however. Adequate demonstration programs need to be devised and those programs showing the most promise tried in a variety of geographic areas and agency settings; the results being compiled and published for parents and professionals. *Legally,* the retarded need a life guardianship program which hopefully will be uniform throughout the United States. The President's Panel presented the case for such guardianship very strongly. Some states (Minnesota, for example) has long had an excellent program. Other states if they do not already have such a program should begin to take steps at once in this direction. As indicated earlier in this chapter the need is especially urgent with the growing number of retardates outliving their parents. Guardianship does not take away any parental rights during the life of the parents but it does protect the retardate once the parents are deceased. A thorough presentation of the need for guardianship may be found in the Report of the Task Force on Law.[9] It is vital that all persons interested in the well being and protection of the retarded should see that adequate comprehensive legislation is passed in every state covering the guardianship contingency. The public is just beginning to understand that the retarded have legal rights as do all other citizens. This

----

[8] Two recent references are suggested: Minnesota Association for Retarded Children: *Survey of Daytime Activity Centers For the Mentally Retarded in Minnesota.* Minneapolis, February, 1965; and Meyer Schreiber: Some basic concepts in social group work and recreation with the mentally retarded. *Rehabilitation Literature,* No. 7, Vol. 26, July, 1965; other work by Meyer Schreiber as editor should also be studied—particularly the various proceedings held by the Association for Help of Retarded Children, New York City.

[9] The President's Panel on Mental Retardation, *Report of the Task Force on Law,* U. S. Department of Health, Education, and Welfare, January, 1963, pp. 24-27.

important area has unfortunately been neglected and the rights of the retarded have not been protected.

Employment. Another goal for the future must be the increasing use of the adult retardate in productive jobs. Until quite recently the concept of the adult retardate as being a possible productive member was looked upon dubiously, if not doubted completely. DiMichael writes that only recently have we understood that retardates with IQ's of 30 can be trained, something which would not have been believed ten years ago.[10] The economic value of training even a limited number of retarded was dramatically stated by Governor Terry Sanford in his talk before the 1963 White House Conference when he pointed out that in 1958 some 1,578 retarded persons completed training under the vocation rehabilitation program. Their earnings before rehabilitation amounted to an annual sum of seventy thousand dollars. After training, these same persons had earnings of 2.5 million dollars or $1,584 per person per year contrasted to the $34.36 per year before training.[11]

The recommendation that full employment opportunities be developed is not only meritorious from the economic viewpoint, but also psychologically and socially desirable for the retardate. Our society has emphasized so thoroughly the college degree and the status of the white collar job that thousands of service jobs go begging—jobs which the retarded could do and would find great satisfaction in doing. The dignity of working with one's hands is a desirable goal which thousands of retardates could understand and appreciate. Around the country there are examples of retarded being trained for useful jobs which serve society and lend dignity to the individual.[12] The future calls for a comprehensive employment training program, not in isolated

---

[10] Salvatore G. DiMichael: The low IQ problem. *Rehabilitation Record,* No. 3, 4:3-6, May-June, 1963.

[11] *The White House Conference on Mental Retardation.* U. S. Department of Health, Education, and Welfare, 1963, p. 35.

[12] The National Association for Retarded Children has begun a three year campaign to promote jobs for the retarded; they are also developing a documentary film for their promotion. Centers such as the Kennedy Center in Bridgeport, Connecticut, are training retardates for jobs; companies such as the W. T. Grant, Co. have adopted policies for hiring the retarded.

instances, but available throughout the country for all retarded.

Also, the future calls for looking at the placement opportunities for the retarded in the following four areas: (a) competitive employment; (b) transitional sheltered employment; (c) long-term sheltered employment, and (d) adult activity center (short or long-term).[13] These classifications remove the stultifying concept of the designations "educable" and "trainable" which are limited in terms of training for employment and reflect the academic approach. DiMichael's call for a change in the use of terms so as to "generate more attention to preparation for adult living"[14] is certainly a long step forward in the right direction, leading hopefully to fuller and more appropriate employment of retarded adolescents and adults.

The goal of full employment opportunities for the retarded will necessitate a life time counseling relationship with employment counselors so that regardless of when a retardate loses a job or if he moves from one state to another, his personnel folder will follow him and contain all pertinent data necessary for continuing employment. Vocational counselors will have to be trained in this specialized work with retardates; the Texas program mentioned previously, although not the only one with such vocational counselors, does indicate a pattern that might be duplicated elsewhere.

Housing. The needs of the adult retarded in regard to housing have in this country received almost no attention until quite recently. Here then is an area of concern for the future that will take some experimentation. If across the country a number of demonstrations of various types of needed housing could be set up, the most promising soon would become evident.

For one thing, it seems that small group homes (small units with minimal care and/or supervision) are especially needed for the adult retardate who is actually on his own but needs some small amount of help. What is being suggested here is a facility that would house probably not more than six or eight persons with minimal supervision being given by a married couple—the

---

[13] Salvatore G. DiMichael: Providing full vocational opportunities for retarded adolescents and adults. *J Rehabilitation,* July-August, 1964, p. 12.

[14] Ibid., pp. 11-14.

wife staying at home while the husband went out to work during the day. This pattern is followed in a number of European countries with evident success. The retarded persons living in this arrangement have similar living accommodation as they would in their own family. It should be noted that this first recommendation is for housing those retarded who are perfectly capable of functioning within the community and is not a temporary half-way house for those moving from institutionalized living back into the community. The housing category may include hostels, foster homes, or small group homes; the essential features however would be the same: a small group living in a family-like arrangement, with the retarded working in the community. This type of housing has greater potential for the individual, and in contrast with mass housing can give him an increased sense of dignity and worth. Other values also accrue to society, benefits both economic and social, when the retarded are able to be substantially "on their own." These values then, both personal and societal, ought to be the motivating force which will make this type of housing available.

PUBLIC INFORMATION

Getting the story before the public requires money and specialists trained in the use of the various media. Nothing is sadder than the parents' association or the agency for the retarded that depends on the "goodwill" of the local newspapers or television to give them coverage. The expected goodwill may be there all right, but the media people have wars, murders, riots, and demonstrations on their minds—also, they must make money. The problems of the retarded, although they loom insurmountably high to the parents, are not in and of themselves *news*. Campaigns then, properly prepared down to the last detail, are necessary to keep in front of the public the needs and the latest developments. The fact is that this must be done dramatically and by professionals who know how to write, know what is required by the news media, and can plan and execute a campaign to put the story across.

Whenever the late President Kennedy spoke about retardation it was "news" and appeared in all the media. The ground swell of interest reflecting his concern, and the tremendously significant production of materials by the President's Panel on Mental Retardation gave the general public more information on retardation and its needs and consequences than had been possible for many years. This momentum may be expected to slack off, and therefore it is necessary to plan ahead in order to gain the maximum benefit from the interest which was created.

Two areas for public information seem to be especially important: (a) the fact that the adult retarded are *handicapped workers* but that nevertheless they can be productive, useful workers and citizens, and (b) the fact that the retarded *although handicapped* have ongoing needs for jobs, education, housing, and employment as well as social and recreational needs.

In respect to the first of these two areas, the National Association for Retarded Children, as previously mentioned, has already taken the first step in educating business and the general public to the idea that it can be good business to hire the mentally retarded. Bringing the retarded under the heading of the *handicapped* has psychological advantages which ought to be utilized. In the United States and most of the civilized world, there is the belief, in some form, that one ought not to kick a man when he is down.[15] Recognition of what is down is especially difficult in regard to mental retardation, and too often the public shrugs off its responsibility by mistakenly identifying retardation as some sort of mental health problem. Fear and confusion are further compounded by the public as the retarded are mistakenly accused of crimes of sex and delinquency. The facts then must be brought to the attention of the public, while at the same time emphasizing that the handicapping condition is not something of which the retardate is *guilty* but instead something which could happen to anyone.

---

[15] The Report of the Task Force on Law of The President's Panel reminds us that in our country we reflect in our laws the Latin expression, *De Minimis non curat Lex*, ". . . [A] *very great and tender consideration for persons naturally disabled* . . ." But, it is still difficult in many cases to know what is just and humane, not to mention the more difficult problem of the law as it relates to recognizing disabilities and differentiating between them.

An information program designed to educate the public to some of the above facts needs to be national in scope and would require the interest and financial assistance of hundreds of units across the country. A concentration of effort then should be centered around the theme of employing the handicapped—why the handicap of mental retardation ought not to be held against the retardate—and from the economic standpoint, why the hiring of the retarded is good business.

In respect to the second of the two areas previously mentioned, public information campaigns need to be directed to the theme that *the handicapped need us and we need them.* The assumption being made here is that the world of work has a number of routine jobs of a simple repetitive nature which the retarded can fill, and in which they will be happy and not seeking constantly for "something more interesting."

The information campaign needs also to emphasize the other aspects—the housing, education, social and recreational needs—in other words, the complete program for the retarded. Mention should be made here of the outstanding job being done by the Kennedy Foundation in the area of general publicity on the problems of the retarded. It would seem that their program, dovetailed with the NARC national and statewide chapters, would serve the ends called for in this chapter. Taking the publicity program right down to the local level would then become an end product.

RESEARCH

A general guide for the future can be found in the *Report of the Task Force on Behavioral and Social Research.*[16] This excellent report deals with each of the following five areas needing additional or continuing research:

(a) Basic behavioral development.

(b) Psychocultural antecedents of intellectual and social disability.

---

[16] The President's Panel on Mental Retardation: *Report of the Task Force on Behavioral and Social Research,* (Ed.) William I. Gardner, U. S. Department of Health, Education, and Welfare, March 1964, p. vii.

(c) Impact of the mentally retarded on the family and on the community.

(d) Services for the mentally retarded.

(e) Brain mechanisms affecting intellectual behavior. The Task Force, in calling attention to these five areas for special emphasis, nevertheless, felt it necessary to point out that it is the general experience of science that breakthroughs of new knowledge are most likely to occur in the broad setting when research is not limited to one discipline.[17] After reviewing the five areas the Task Force expressed as its view that the area most likely to lead to a significant understanding of mental retardation would be research directed to exploration of ". . . the development and maturation of the nervous system and of behavior."[18] And, finally that ". . . it would seem of the greatest importance to direct attention equivalently to measures for advancing, increasing, and improving brain function and mental performance."[19]

In arriving at the above conclusions, the Task Force focused on the all important matter of prevention and increased function, goals much to be desired by all. Certainly research must be directed to this area, and the writer does not want to be misunderstood in directing the reader to an equally important area: sociological and psychological studies of the family of the retardate. The scarcity of useful studies has already been mentioned. Mothers are particularly affected since the care of the retardate most often falls directly upon them. Our knowledge of *what helps* is a spotty and chance thing lacking the systemization resulting from rigidly controlled research studies. This gap in our practice knowledge so important in the field of social work needs attention along with the emphasis on prevention and increased function. Social workers, public health nurses, physicians, and others in the helping professions need tested practice knowledge which can be used to help mothers, fathers and the other family members. This type of knowledge is needed in

---

[17] *Ibid.*, p. 52.
[18] *Ibid.*
[19] *Ibid.*

addition to the broad knowledge required regarding retardation itself.

The Task Force report in discussing *Impact on the Family* makes clear that research in this area will challenge the best that sociologists and social psychologists have to offer. The fact that the report does not mention any possible contribution from the field of social work reflects in part the limited professional concern by social work researchers of the impact of retardation on the family.

The suggestion here is for a closer working relationship of those in the helping professions, schools of social work, and those interested in research. Crossing disciplinary lines as suggested earlier may result in creative new solutions and practice knowledge.

A PROGRAM OF ACTION

The report to the President by the President's Panel on Mental Retardation will undoubtedly contain for some time to come the essential outlines of the areas towards which we must direct our attention.[20] The summary of the eight main recommendations regarding research and prevention, and the four additional recommendations can be found in the appendix of this book and should be studied carefully by agency executives, parents, professionals, and others interested in progress. The report to the President and the reports of the various Task Forces taken together form the most comprehensive look at retardation problems now available.

The action program recommended to the President is basically aimed at the federal level, although statewide and local implications are recognized. The Council of State Governments, for example, concurred with the President's Panel in recommending that every agency of state government involved in attention to the retarded should have at least one person (if not an office) with specialized knowledge about the retarded and their needs, with the authority to stimulate action, able to work collabora-

---

[20] *Op. cit.*, pp. 14-15.

tively across departmental lines, and able to devote full time to this work.

We know that few states have reached a decision as to which department should be responsible; many do not have as yet a person whose sole duty is to work for the interests of the retarded. In some states the program should probably be under public welfare; in others, under public health or public institutions These are details which need attention. Units of NARC working cooperatively with state and federal officials can find the best solution for each state.

Much that has been going on at the federal level in the Departments of Health, Education, and Welfare is especially hopeful. The recent assignment of responsibility by HEW to a new Mental Retardation Branch (under the Bureau of States Services, USPHS) means that there is now a branch of the federal government whose sole responsibility is the promotion of services to the mentally retarded. This in an important step forward for the coordination of federal services.

Continued pressure, however, will be necessary at the local level and here small units of interested citizens can probably accomplish a great deal. Necessary legislation, funds to provide services, agitation for programs that will benefit parents and especially mothers—all of these things fall upon the interested citizen as part of his responsibility. There is much to be done, and fortunately for the retardate's future it looks as though there is interest enough in the United States, so that much will be done.

APPENDIX

TABLE VIII
CHARACTERISTICS OF THE FAMILIES

Case Number	Age Husband	Age Wife	Social Class	Marriage Years	"Take Home" Income	Religion Cath.	Religion Prot.	White	Colored	8th Grade or less Fa.	8th Grade or less Mo.	Some High School Fa.	Some High School Mo.	High School Grad Fa.	High School Grad Mo.	High School + Fa.	High School + Mo.	College Grad Fa.	College Grad Mo.	No. of Children	Age of Retardate
1	28	27	U-L	5	$4472	x		x		x			x							3	5.7
2	46	42	L-M	12	6240	x		x			x				x	x				3	5.0
3	36	34	L-L	14	3328		x		x						x					7	5.0
4	34	32	U-L	13	2860	x		x		x	x									5	7.1
5	40	38	U-L	10	3900	x		x			x			x						5	2.7
6	29	29	L-M	10	4680	x		x						x	x					5	5.10
7	33	30	L-M	10	4800		x	x						x	x					6	7.8
8	45	44	L-M	15	3640	x		x			x			x						4	3.10
9	44	42	U-L	13	4200	x		x		x	x									3	5.1
10	37	34	L-M	11	6760	x		x						x	x	x				3	4.9
11	42	43	L-M	8	5400[1]		x	x						x	x					2	3.4
12	40	40	U-L	15	4420[2]	x			x	x	x									3	4.4
13	34	35	L-M	12	4000[3]	x		x								x	x			3	5.0
14	31	33	U-L	11	3796	x		x					x			x				3	5.11
15	38	38	L-M	5	4200		x	x				x						x	x	5	6.0
16	37	43	U-L	15	3900	x		x				x	x							3	2.0
17	28	22	L-L	9	3380	x		x		x	x		x							3	3.1
18	38	31	U-L	10	4160[2]		x	x		x							x			1	9.7
19	51	47	L-M	11	2760	x		x								x	x			3	8.6
20	39	33	U-M	10	5640	x		x				x				x	x	x		5	7.6
21	43	40	L-M	15	4420[3]	x		x			x	x	x							7	7.2
22	51	48	L-L	26	2511	x		x		x	x	x	x							4	7.10
23	42	34	L-L	9	2704	x		x						x			x			3	5.3
24	31	36	L-M	10	4320	x		x						x	x					3	9.7
	Av. 42.4	Av. 36.4		Av. 11.6	Median $4180	19	5	22	2	6	7	3	5	9	6	4	5	2	1	88	Av. 5.7

Code: If Catholic mother, family classified as Catholic unless mother has stated otherwise.
Italicized numbers = family separated.
[1] = $60/month to first wife.
[2] = Father unemployed at time of study. Income shown if working full time.
[3] = Low rent; father owns house.

133

TABLE IX*

ORGANIZATION AND CLASSIFICATION OF INSTRUCTIONAL GROUPS

No.	Classification	IQ	Educational Category	Social and Occupational Prognosis
1	Borderline	70-84	Educable Slow learner	Independent
2	Mild	55-69	Educable	Independent
3	Moderate	40-54	Trainable	Semi-dependent
4	Severe	25-39	Trainable Residential	Semi-dependent Dependent
5	Profound	0-24	Residential	Dependent

* Report of the Task Force on Education and Rehabilitation, President's Panel on Mental Retardation, U. S. Department of Health, Education and Welfare, 1962.

DATA GUIDE

Interview ....

Informant ....

Date ....

A. WHAT KINDS OF BEHAVIOR OF THE CHILD ARE RE-
LATED TO THE MOTHERS SUSPECTING MENTAL RE-
TARDATION?

1. Description of specific behavior observed by mothers which
   raised some questions regarding normalcy. ("Lack of response"
   type behavior?)
2. What is the typical pattern of behavior?
3. What specific behavior pattern was instrumental in causing
   mothers to seek medical or other advice?
4. How long did mothers wait before taking action (after the
   suspicious behavior) to go to a clinic or to other persons for
   further diagnosis, confirmation, etc.?
5. Was there a period of "watchful waiting," of shock or im-
   mobilization regarding the next step?
6. Was the behavior of the child questioned or commented upon
   by any of the relatives, neighbors, friends, medical, or other
   professional persons prior to the parents' decision to investi-
   gate further?

B. WHAT TYPES OF PERSONS HAVE CONSPICUOUS INFLU-
ENCE ON THE MOTHERS BRINGING (OR NOT BRINGING)
THE CHILD TO AN AGENCY GIVING SERVICE TO THE
MENTALLY RETARDED?

1. When the behavior of the child raised questions in the minds
   of the mothers, to whom did they turn for (a) discussion of the
   problem, (b) for suggestions as to action or "what to do" about
   it?
2. What types of persons were sought out? Neighbors, friends,
   relatives, professionals, etc.? How sought out and why?

3. What did these persons advise or suggest?
4. What advice or suggestion was reported as having helped them make a decision one way or the other?
5. Regarding the suspicion of mental retardation—do the mothers mention the neighbors, friends, relatives, etc. as being or not being helpful regarding their problem? Do they more often mention professional types of persons?
6. Specifically, what type or types of persons are reported as having led the family to bring the child to the CSRC? Or— did parents come on their own motivation without reference to others?

C. WHAT SERVICES ARE OFFERED AND RENDERED BY A SPECIALIZED COMMUNITY AGENCY FOR MENTALLY RE-TARDED CHILDREN AND THEIR FAMILIES?

1. What specific services were recommended by the agency?
2. What services were actually rendered the family and/or the child?

D. WHAT SERVICES WERE USED BY THE FAMILIES?

1. What services did the parents accept as "wanted?"
2. What services did the parents reject?
3. What services do the parents want which (a) have not been offered, or (b) are not available?

E. WHAT SERVICES DO MOTHERS REPORT AS ALLEVIAT-ING OR MODIFYING THE PROBLEMS THEY FACED?

1. Regarding the child—what specific problems do the mothers report as being alleviated or modified?
2. Do the mothers report concrete help with their problems? Specify. How did the service help—in what way—and WHY do they think it helped?
3. Regarding the mothers—what specific problems do the parents report as alleviated or modified? (Note especially problems of anxiety, fear, conflict, frustration, stigma, etc.)
4. What expectations did the mothers have regarding services?
5. Have the mothers "told the whole story" or have they attempted to "hold back" criticism of themselves, the services, or the staff?
6. What do mothers see as future needs or problems that will need service?
7. What "helps" mothers (not necessarily agency services)?

FAMILY CHARACTERIZED BY THE FOLLOWING:

F. **Regarding Action**
1. Passiveness (will accept any suggestion without any real enthusiasm). Describe.
2. Aggressiveness (fighting for action, services, etc.). Describe.
3. Immobilized (regarding possible action). Describe.

G. **Housing**
1. Slum conditions (run down, disorder, lowest type housing). Describe.
2. Average lower class. Describe (clean, neat, or?).
3. Middle class. Describe.
4. Upper class. Describe.

H. **Siblings**
1. Other sibs with problems?
2. Problems caused by retarded sib.
3. Other sibs aggravating retardate's problem?

I. **Illness and Medical Care**
1. Illness, somatic—below average for most of family— Describe.
2. Illness, somatic—about average for most of family— Describe.
3. Illness, somatic—above average for most of family— Describe.
4. Illness, mental, emotional—Describe.
5. Medical care by family doctor, specialist, city hosiptal, or?
6. Degree of satisfaction with medical services.

J. **Educational Level**
1. Father's level of education.
2. Mother's level of education.
3. General level of other sibs

K. **Socioeconomic Status**
1. Father employed as ....
2. Father's economic or cultural or educational aspirations?
3. Mother employed as ....
4. Mother's economic, cultural or educational aspirations?
5. Mother at home? Father at home? Both?
6. General cultural level of the family as evidenced by literature, music, art, language, etc.

L. **Religious Participation**
   1. Church membership—active, average, minimal, inactive.
   2. Role of religion as seen by family of retardate (e.g., see religion as rationalizing mental retardation? etc.).
   3. Affiliation—Protestant, Jewish, Catholic, other.

M. **Knowledge Regarding Mental Retardation**
   1. Degree of knowledge regarding etiology of retardation.
   2. How does family define mental retardation?
   3. Knowledge regarding future of retardate (limits, abilities, etc.).

N. **Reality Impact**
   1. Parents aware of reality problems facing family.
   2. Ambivalent attitudes.
   3. Family can (cannot) face continuing existence of retardate at home.
   4. Family has adapted its life pattern to include (exclude) retardate.
   5. Sibs are aware (unaware) of actual conditions of retardate.
   6. Parents agree (disagree) regarding care, treatment of retardate.

O. **Family Self Image**
   1. Class position: Does family see itself as lower, middle, or upper class?
   2. Coping ability: Does family see itself as able or unable, to handle retardate?
   3. Attitude: Does family see itself as hostile, fearful, resigned, or hopeful regarding the retardate?

P. **Family Composition**
   1. Retardate living with natural family.
   2. Natural father is in the home.
   3. Natural mother is in the home.
   4. Extended family, relatives, others living in the home.
   5. Family broken by death, divorce or other.

Q. **Emotional Patterns**
   1. Family exhibits evidences of stigma, shame, guilt, love, towards the retardate. (As evidenced through such objective behavior as taking or not taking child out to visit, care and attention paid, attempts at teaching, attempts to hide child, etc.)

R. **Background Data**
   1. Patient—date of birth, where, when, what conditions at time of birth, etc.

2. Birthdates: Father
   Mother
   Siblings
3. Sex of retardate.
   Sex of siblings.
4. Birth order of retardate—Specify all sibs.
5. Color or race: White
   Negro
   Oriental
   American Indian
   Other

S. **Behavioral Data**

1. Responsiveness: Behavior in accord with or superior to expectations re age level
   Slight but significant deficiency (according to one or more criteria)
   Moderate but definite deficiency (according to one or more criteria)
   Severely deficient (according to one or more criteria)
2. Motor skills (see above four points).
3. Auditory skills (see above four points).
4. Visual skills (see above four points).
5. Speech skills (see above four points).
6. Ambulation: Ambulatory
   Partially ambulatory
   Nonambulatory
7. Toilet-training: Completely tidy
   Tidy except for nocturnal enuresis
   Partially tidy (some daytime untidiness)
8. Eating skills: Feeds self completely
   Feeds self partially
   Does not feed self
9. Dressing skills: Dresses self completely
   Dresses self partially
   Does not dress self

T. **Economic status of family**

Family fully dependent on public support.
Family partially dependent on public support.
Family receiving no public assistance but total annual income under $2,000.

Total annual income $2,000 to $3,999
Total annual income 4,000 to 5,999
Total annual income 6,000 to 7,999
Total annual income 8,000 to 9,999
Total annual income 10,000 or greater

U. **Number of Living Siblings—Specify.**

V. **Sibling Behavior.**

All siblings have history of average or better social adjustment.

One or more siblings has history of average or better social adjustment.

One or more siblings has history of subaverage social adjustment.

One or more siblings has history of mental retardation.

One or more siblings has history of mental illness or emotional disturbance.

One or more siblings has history of delinquent or anti-social behavior.

One or more siblings has history of one or more years of educational retardation.

One or more siblings has history of average or better educational achievement.

All siblings have history of average or better educational achievement.

W. **Age of Parents at Time of Patient's Birth—Mother**
                                                   Father

X. **Personal-Social History of Father and Mother**

No history of personal or social maladjustment.

History of criminal or antisocial behavior.

History of emotional instability.

Mentally retarded.

History of mental illness.

Unknown.

Data pertains to substitute father or mother.

For interviewer:

    1. Immediate impressions of family. Relationship with patient. Attitude toward interviewer—friendly, cooperative, unfriendly, etc.

    2. Supplementary coding: Class aspirations apparent? Indicative of class level? Striving upward? Satisfaction with status?
       Intensity of ethnic identification.
       Use of leisure time?
       Noticeable deviant behavior?

RECOMMENDATIONS OF THE
PRESIDENT'S PANEL*

THE PANEL RECOGNIZES that extreme shortages of trained personnel and funds will not make it possible to increase services and facilities greatly overnight. We must plan our campaign to combat mental retardation not for just next month or next year, but for the next decade. And we must move ahead vigorously and imaginatively. In this context, the main recommendations of the report are directed to

(a) *Research* in the causes of retardation and in methods of care, rehabilitation, and learning.

(b) *Preventive health measures* including a greatly strengthened program of maternal and infant care directed first at the centers of population where prematurity and the rate of "damaged" children are high; protection against such known hazards to pregnancy as radiation and harmful drugs, and extended diagnostic and screening services.

(c) *Strengthened educational programs generally and extended and enriched programs of special education* in public and private schools closely coordinated with vocational guidance, vocational rehabilitation, and specific training and preparation for employment; education for the adult mentally retarded, and workshops geared to their needs.

(d) *More comprehensive and improved clinical and social services.*

(e) *Improved methods and facilities for care,* with emphasis

---

* Adapted from, The President's Panel on Mental Retardation, a Proposed Program for National Action to Combat Mental Retardation, U. S. Government Printing Office, Washington, D. C., October 1962, pp. 14-15.

on the home and the development of a wide range of local community facilities.

(f) *A new legal, as well as social, concept of the retarded,* including protection of their civil rights; life guardianship provisions when needed; an enlightened attitude on the part of the law and the courts, and clarification of the theory of responsibility in criminal acts.

(g) *Helping overcome the serious problems of manpower* as they affect the entire field of science and every type of service through extended programs of recruiting with fellowships, and increased opportunities for graduate students, and those preparing for the professions to observe and learn at firsthand about the phenomenon of retardation. Because there will never be a fully adequate supply of personnel in this field, and for other cogent reasons, the panel has emphasized the need for more volunteers in health, recreation, and welfare activities, and for a domestic Peace Corps to stimulate voluntary service.

(h) *Programs of education and information to increase public awareness* of the problem of mental retardation.

In addition to a strong emphasis on *research* and *prevention,* the report recommends (1) that programs for the retarded, including modern day care, recreation, residential services, and ample education and vocational opportunities, be *comprehensive;* (2) that they operate in or close to the communities where the retarded live—that is, that they be *community centered;* (3) that services be so organized as to provide a central or fixed point for the guidance, assistance, and protection of retarded persons if and when needed, and to assure a sufficient array or *continuum* of services to meet different types of need, and (4) that private, as well as public, agencies at the local, state, and federal level continue to provide resources and to increase them for this worthy purpose. While the federal government can assist, the principal responsibility for financing and improving services for the mentally retarded must continue to be borne by states and local communities.

SELECTED BIBLIOGRAPHY

AINSWORTH, MARY D., *et al.*: *Deprivation of Maternal Care; A Reassessment of Its Effects.* Geneva, World Health Organization, 1962.

AMERICAN ASSOCIATION ON MENTAL DEFICIENCY: A Manual on Terminology and Classification in Mental Retardation. Supplement to *Amer J Ment Defic,* September, 1959.

APPELL, MELVILLE V., WILLIAMS, CLARENCE M., AND FISHELL, KENNETH N.: Changes in attitudes of parents of retarded children effected through group counseling. *Amer J Ment Defic,* Vol. 68, No. 6, May, 1964.

APTEKAR, HERBERT H: *The Dynamics of Casework and Counseling.* New York, Houghton Mifflin Co., 1955.

AUSUBEL, D. P., *et al.*: Perceived parent attitudes as determinants of children's ego structure. *Child Develop, 25,* 1954.

BARCLAY, A., GOULET, L. R., HOLTGREWE, M. M., AND SHARP, A. R.: Parental evaluation of clinical services for retarded children. *Amer J Ment Defic,* Vol. 67, No. 2, pp. 232-237, 1962.

BECK, HELEN L.: Counseling parents of retarded children. *Children,* Vol. 6, No. 6, November-December, 1959.

BEGAB, MICHAEL J.: Factors in counseling parents of retarded children, *Amer J Ment Defic, 515:524,* January, 1956.

————————:Unmet needs of the mentally retarded in the community. *Amer J Ment Defic,* No. 4, 62:712-23, January, 1958.

————————: Child-welfare service for the mentally retarded. *Children,* May-June, 1958.

————————: A social work approach to the mentally retarded and their families. *Amer J Ment Defic,* Vol. 63, No. 3, p. 524, November, 1958.

————————: Some basic considerations in casework with mentally retarded children and their families. Address given before Field Services Staff, Bureau of Mental Deficiency, New Jersey. Circulated in mimeographed form by U. S. Dept. of Health, Education, and Welfare.

————————: *The Mentally Retarded Child—A Guide to Services of Social Agencies.* Publication No. 404. Published by U. S. Dept. of Health, Education, and Welfare, Children's Bureau, 1963.

BELINKOFF, CORNELIA: Community attitudes toward mental retardation. *Amer J Ment Defic*, Vol. 65, No. 2, pp. 221-226, 1960.

BELL, NORMAN, TRIESCHMAN, ALBERT, AND VOGEL, EZRA: A sociocultural analysis of the resistances of working class fathers treated in a child psychiatric clinic. A mimeographed advance copy of material which is part of a broader study, "The Influence of the Family and Cultural Values on the Mental Health and Illness of the Individual."

BELL, NORMAN, AND VOGEL, EZRA F.: *The Family.* Glencoe, Free Press, 1960.

BENDA, CLEMENS E.: "Mongolism—A Comprehensive Review," *Archives of Pediatrics*, 73:391-407, 1956.

BOGGS, ELIZABETH: State programming for the mentally deficient. *Community Organization*, New York, Columbia University Press, 1958.

BOWMAN, PETER W., AND MAUTNER, HANS V.: *Mental Retardation.* Proceedings of the First International Medical Conference at Portland, Maine.

BREITENBECK, G.: *For Parents of Retarded Children.* Missouri, Liguorian Pamphlets, Redemptorist Fathers.

BUCK, PEARL S.: *The Child Who Never Grew.* New York, John Day Co., 1950.

BUCKLEY, RITA MARY: "Casework With Families of Five Mental Retardates Institutionalized at the Walter E. Fernald State School." Master's Thesis, Boston College, 1959.

CALDWELL, BETTYE M., MANLEY, E. V., AND NISSAW, Y. N.: Reactions of community agencies and parents to services provided in a clinic for retarded children. *Amer J Ment Defic*, 65:582-589, 1961.

CALDWELL, BETTYE M., MANLEY, E. J., AND SEELYE, BARBARA J.: Factors associated with parental reactions to a clinic for retarded children. *Amer J Ment Defic*, 65:590-594, 1961.

CALIFORNIA COUNCIL FOR RETARDED CHILDREN: *Financial Assistance Available for the Mentally Retarded in California.* Sacramento, The Council, 1107 - 9th St., N.D.

CAMBRIDGE PLANNING BOARD STAFF: *Thirteen Neighborhoods: One City.* Cambridge, Mass., Cambridge City Council, 1954.

————————: *Reference Data, Cambridge, Mass.:* Cambridge, Cambridge Planning Board, 1954.

CAMBRIDGE SERVICE FOR RETARDED CHILDREN: *Annual Report to the Children's Bureau,* for the period July 1, 1959 - June 30, 1960. Cambridge, Cambridge Service for Retarded Children, 1960.

CARTER, JOHN: A social work approach to the mentally retarded and their families. *Amer J Ment Defic,* p. 529, November, 1958.

CAUDILL, WILLIAM, AND ROBERTS, BERTRAM A.: Pitfalls in the organization of interdisciplinary research. In Adams, Richard N., and Preiss, Jack J. (Ed): *Human Organization Research,* Homewood, Illinois, The Dorsey Press, 1960.

CHINOY, ELY: *Sociological Perspective.* New York, Random House, 1954.

CLAUSEN, JOHN A., AND YARROW, MARIAN R.: Paths to the mental hospital. *The Journal of Social Issues,* Vol. 11, No. 4, 1955.

COTTRELL, LEONARD S.: Some neglected problems in social psychology. *Amer Sociol Rev,* 1950.

COUNCIL OF STATE GOVERNMENTS: *Action in the States in the Field of Mental Health, Mental Retardation and Related Areas; A Report on Recent Financial, Legal and Administrative Developments in the States' Mental Health Programs.* Chicago, Interstate Clearing House on Mental Health, 1963.

COUNCIL ON SOCIAL WORK EDUCATION: *Public Health Concepts in Social Work Education.* Proceedings of Seminar Held at Princeton University, Princeton, New Jersey, 1962.

DAVIES, STANLEY POWELL (WITH THE COLLABORATION OF ECOB, KATHERINE G.: *The Mentally Retarded in Society.* New York, Columbia University Press, 1959.

DEASY, LEILA CALHOUN, AND QUINN, OLIVE WESTBROOKE: The wife of the mental patient and the hospital psychiatrist. *The Journal of Social Issues,* Issue Editors: Clausen, John A., and Yarrow, Marian Radke, Vol. 11, No. 4, 1955.

DIMICHAEL, SALVATORE G.: The low IQ problem. *Rehabilitation Record,* Vol. 4, No. 3, pp. 3-6, May-June, 1963.

DITTMAN, LAURA L.: *The Mentally Retarded Child at Home.* Washington, U. S. Dept. of Health, Education, and Welfare, Social Security Admin., Children's Bureau, 1959.

DRAYER, CARL, AND SCHLESINGER, ELFRIEDE G.: The informing interview. *Amer J Ment Defic,* 65:363-370, No. 3, November, 1960.

DUHL, LEONARD J.: The normal development of the retarded child. *Amer J Ment Defic,* 62:585, No. 4, January, 1958.

DURLING, DOROTHY, AND BENDA, CLEMENS E.: Mental growth curves in untreated institutionalized mongoloid patients. *Amer J Ment Defic,* Vol. 56, No. 3, January, 1952.

DYBWAD, GUNNAR: *Challenges in Mental Retardation.* New York, Columbia University Press, 1964.

——————: Community organization for the mentally retarded. *Community Organization.* New York, Columbia University, 1959.

——————: Mental retardation. In Kurtz, Russell H. (Ed.): *Social Work Yearbook, 1960,* New York, National Association of Social Workers, 1960.

FAMILY SERVICE ASSOCIATION OF AMERICA: *Casework Services for Parents of Handicapped Children.* Ten papers reprinted from *Social Casework,* New York, the Association, 1964.

FARBER, BERNARD: Effects of a severely mentally retarded child on family integration. *Monograph—Society for Research in Child Development,* Vol. 24, No. 2, 1959.

——————: Family organization and crisis: maintenance of integration in families with a severely mentally retarded child. *Monograph —Society for Research in Child Development,* Vol. 25, No. 1, 1960.

——————: Perceptions of crisis and related variables in the impact of a retarded child on the mother. *J Health Hum Behav,* No. 2, *I*:108-118, Summer, 1960.

FARRELL, MALCOLM J.: The adverse effects of early institutionalization of mentally subnormal children. *American Medical Association Journal of Diseases of Children,* Vol. 91, March, 1956.

FERNALD, WALTER E.: The history of the treatment of the feeble-minded. *Proceedings of the National Conference of Charities and Correction, 1893.* Boston, Geo. H. Ellis Press, 1893.

FOSS, BRIAN M. (Ed.): *Tavistock Seminar on Mother-Infant Inter-action.* London, 1959-1961.

——————: *Determinants of Infant Behavior; Proceedings.* London, Methuen, 1961-63.

FOSTER, HELEN B.: *Services in Public Assistance, The Role of the Caseworker.* Washington, U. S. Dept. of Health, Education, and Welfare, Public Assistance Report 30, N.D.

FREEDMAN, ALFRED, *et al.*: Family adjustment to the brain-damaged child, in *The Family,* by Bell, Norman W., and Vogel, Ezra F., Glencoe, Free Press, 1960.

FREEMAN, HOWARD E.: Attitudes toward mental illness among relatives of former patients. *Amer Sociol Rev,* Vol. 26, No. 1, February, 1961.

FREEMAN, RUTH B.: *Public Health Nursing Practice.* Philadelphia, W. B. Saunders Co., 1957.

FRIEDSON, ELIOT: Specialties without roots: the utilization of new services. *Human Organization,* Vol. 18, N.D.

FRENCH, EDWARD L., AND SCOTT, W. CLIFFORD: *Child in the Shadows: A Manual for Parents of Retarded Children.* Philadelphia, Lippincott, 1960.

GARFIELD, SOL L., AND HALPER, M. M.: Parental attitudes and socioeconomic status. *J Clin Psychol,* No. 18, pp. 171-175, 1962.

GORDON, MILTON M.: *Social Class in American Sociology.* Durham, Duke Univ. Press, 1958.

GRALIKER, BETTY V., PARMALEE, SR., ARTHUR H., AND KOCH, RICHARD: Attitude study of parents of mentally retarded children. *Pediatrics,* No. 5, *24*:819-21, November, 1958.

GURIN, GERALD, VEROFF, JOSEPH, AND FELD, SHEILA: *Americans View Their Mental Health.* New York, Basic Books, 1960.

HEBER, RICK: Modifications in the manual on terminology and classification in mental retardation. *Amer J Ment Defic,* Vol. 65, No. 4, January, 1961.

HILL, REUBEN C., *et al.: Families Under Stress.* New York, Harper and Bros., 1949.

HILL, REUBEN C.: Generic features of families under stress. *Social Casework, 39*:139-150, 1958.

HOLLINGSHEAD, AUGUST B., AND REDLICH, FREDERICK C.: *Social Class and Mental Illness.* New York, John Wiley and Sons, 1958.

HOLTGREWE, MARIAN M.: *A Guide for Public Health Nurses Working with Mentally Retarded Children.* Washington, U. S. Dept. of Health, Education, and Welfare, 1964.

HORMUTH, RUDOLF P.: *Clinical Programs for Mentally Retarded Children, A Listing.* Washington, U. S. Dept. of Health, Education, and Welfare, 1965.

———————: *The Public Health Nurse in Community Planning for the Mentally Retarded.* U. S. Dept. of Health, Education, and Welfare, Social Security Administration, Children's Bureau, 1957.

———————: The problems of mental retardation. *Public Health News,* Vol. 41, No. 9, September, 1960.

HORWITZ, JOHN J.: *Education for Social Workers in the Rehabilitation of the Handicapped.* Vol 8, New York, Council on Social Work Education.

JOHNSON, DAGNEY: The social worker's role in helping the brain-injured child. *Amer J Ment Defic,* p. 419, October, 1956.

JOHNSON, GERTRUDE: The public health nurse and the mentally retarded child. *Public Health News,* New Jersey State Dept. of Health, Vol. 31, No. 9, September, 1960.

JOHNSON, W.: *People in Quandaries.* New York, Harper and Bros., 1946.

KAPLAN, MILTON, AND HINGELEY, HAZEL: A study of the out-patient clinic services for the mentally retarded at the Muscatatuck State School. *Amer J Ment Defic,* No. 3, *63*:517-523, November, 1958.

KATZ, ALFRED H.: *Parents of the Handicapped.* Springfield, Charles C Thomas, 1961.

KELMAN, HOWARD R.: Individualizing the social integration of the mentally retarded child. *Amer J Ment Defic,* No. 4, *60*:860-866, April, 1956.

——————: Some problems in casework with parents of mentally retarded children. *Amer J Ment Defic,* p. 595, January, 1957.

KIRK, SAMUEL ALEXANDER, KARNES, MERLE B., AND KIRK, WINIFRED D.: *You and Your Retarded Child.* New York, Macmillan, 1955.

KOHN, MELVIN L.: Social class and parental values. *Amer J Sociol,* Vol. 64, 1959.

KOOS, EARL LOMON: *Families in Trouble.* New York, King's Crown Press, 1946.

KONOPKA, GISELA: "Through Group Work: Reaching Disadvantaged Youth," Paper given at the Second Institute on Counseling Disadvantaged Youth, No. 19, 1964. Printed in *Minnesota Welfare,* Spring, 1965.

KRAMM, ELIZABETH ROSE: *The Mongolian Child and His Family.* Doctoral Dissertation, Univ. of Pittsburgh Graduate School of Public Health, Pittsburgh, Pa., 1958.

LANDY, DAVID: *Problems of the Person Seeking Help in Our Culture.* New York, Columbia Univ. Press, 1960, pp. 127-145.

LEMKAU, P. V., TIETZE, C., AND COOPER, M.: Mental health problems in an urban district. *Ment Hyg,* 26:275-288, 1942.

LEVINSON, ABRAHAM: *The Mentally Retarded Child.* New York, John Day Co., 1952.

LEVINSON, ABRAHAM, AND BIGLER, JOHN A.: *Mental Retardation in Infants and Children.* Chicago, Year Book Publishers, Inc., 1960.

LEVY, JOSEPH H.: A study of parent groups for handicapped children. *Exceptional Children,* No. 1, *19*:19-26, 1952.

LUSZKI, MARGARET BARRON: *Interdisciplinary Team Research: Methods and Problems.* Washington, National Training Laboratories, New York Univ. Press, 1958.

MACCOBY, ELEANOR E., AND MACCOBY, NATHAN: "The Interview: A Tool of Social Science," in *Handbook of Social Psychology.* Cambridge, Addison-Wesley Publishing Co., Inc., 1954.

MASLAND, RICHARD L., SARASON, SEYMOUR B., AND GLADWIN, THOMAS: *Mental Subnormality.* New York, Basic Books, Inc., 1958.

MAYER, KURT B.: (Rev. Ed.) *Class and Society.* New York, Random House, 1955.

MEYER, HENRY V., AND BORGATTA, EDGAR F.: *An Experiment in Mental Patient Rehabilitation*: *Evaluating a Social Agency Program.* New York, Russell Sage Foundation, 1959.

MILLER, WALTER B.: Implications of urban lower-class culture for social work. *The Social Service Review,* Vol. 33, No. 3, November, 1959.

MILLS, C. WRIGHT: *White Collar.* New York, Oxford University Press, 1956.

MINNEAPOLIS ASSOCIATION FOR RETARDED CHILDREN: *Training Institute*: *A Report.* Minneapolis, August-September, 1964.

MINNESOTA ASSOCIATION FOR RETARDED CHILDREN, INC.: *Survey of Daytime Activity Centers for the Mentally Retarded in Minnesota.* Minneapolis, The Association, February, 1965.

MINNESOTA MENTAL RETARDATION PLANNING COUNCIL: *Working Papers on Mental Retardation*: *Project Proposal.* St. Paul. Morris Hursh, Commissioner, Minnesota Dept. of Public Welfare, 1965.

MURRAY, DOROTHY: Needs of parents of mentally retarded children. *Amer J Ment Defic,* No. 6, *63*:1078-1088, May, 1959.

MYERS, JEROME K., AND ROBERTS, BERTRAM H.: *Family and Class Dynamics in Mental Illness.* New York, John Wiley and Sons, Inc., 1959.

NADAL, ROBERT M.: A counseling program for parents of severely retarded preschool children. *Social Casework,* No. 2, *42*:78-83, February, 1961.

PARAD, HOWARD J., AND CAPLAN, GERALD: A framework for studying families in crisis. *Social Work,* No. 3, *5*:3-15, July 1960.

PARSONS, TALCOTT: *The Social System.* See especially Chapter VII— "Deviant Behavior and the Mechanisms of Social Control." Glencoe, The Free Press, 1951.

Public Health News, Vol. 31, No. 9, September, 1960. Trenton, The New Jersey State Dept. of Health.

RAINWATER, LEE, COLEMAN, RICHARD P., AND HANDEL, GERALD: *Workingman's Wife.* New York, Oceana Publications, Inc., 1959.

Report No. 43, Basic Considerations in Mental Retardation: *A Preliminary Report.* New York, Group for the Advancement of Psychiatry, 1959.

RIDENOUR, NINA: *Mental Health in the United States, a Fifty-year History*. Cambridge, Harvard Univ. Press, 1961.

SAENGER, GERHART: *Factors Influencing the Institutionalization of Mentally Retarded Individuals in New York City*. New York, New York State Interdepartmental Health Resources Board, January, 1960.

SARASON, SEYMOUR B.: *Psychological Problems in Mental Deficiency*. New York, Harper and Bros., 1953.

——————: Psychological and cultural problems in mental subnormality: a review of research. *Amer J Ment Defic*, p. 293, October, 1954.

SCASZ, THOMAS S.: The uses of naming and the origin of the myth of mental illness. *Amer Psychol*, No. 2, *61*:59, 65, February, 1961.

SCHONNEL, F. J., AND WATTS, B. H.: A first survey of the effects of a subnormal child in the family unit. *Amer J Ment Defic*, No. 1, *61*:210-219, July, 1956.

SCHREIBER, MEYER: Some basic concepts in social group work and recreation with the mentally retarded. *Rehabilitation Literature*, No. 7, *26*:194-203, July, 1965.

SCHULMAN, J. L., AND STERN, S.: Parents' estimate of the intelligence of retarded children. *Amer J Ment Defic*, *63*:696, 1959.

SCHWARTZ, MORRIS S.: "Social Research in the Mental Hospital," *Social Perspectives on Behavior*. Glencoe, The Free Press, 1959.

SELIGMAN, EDWIN R. A., AND JOHNSON, ALVIN: *Encyclopaedia of the Social Sciences*. X—"Mental Defectives." New York, The Macmillan Co., 1933, pp. 312-313.

SHUMAN, ANN GOLDSMITH: *Maternal Attitudes Towards the Problem of Mental Retardation*. Master's Thesis, Boston University, School of Social Work, 1960.

SIEGEL, SIDNEY: *Nonparametric Statistics for the Behavioral Sciences*. New York, McGraw-Hill, 1956.

SIMMONS, OZZIE G.: "The Clinical Team in a Chilean Health Center," *Health, Culture, and Community*. New York, Russell Sage Foundation, 1955.

SLAUGHTER, STELLA STILLSON: *The Mentally Retarded Child and His Parent*. New York, Harper and Bros., 1960.

STANTON, ALFRED H., AND SCHWARTZ, MORRIS S.: *The Mental Hospital*. New York, Basic Books, 1954.

STATE OF CALIFORNIA, DEPT. OF MENTAL HYGIENE: "Help and Hope for Retarded," *California Mental Health Progress*, Vol. 6, No. 1, January, 1965.

——————: "The Bold Approach," *California Mental Health Prgress,* Vol. 6, No. 1, January, 1965.

STONE, MARGUERITE M.: Parental attitudes to retardation. *Amer J Ment Defic, 53*:363-372, 1948.

TIZARD, J.: Public health aspects of severe mental subnormality. *Roy Soc Health J,* No. 4, *80*:327-331, July-August, 1960.

TRUEDLEY, MARY B.: Mental illness and family routines. *Ment Hyg, 30*:235-249, 1946.

TULANE UNIVERSITY, SCHOOL OF SOCIAL WORK (Elizabeth Wisner, Dean): *Newer Concepts of Mental Retardation in Medical Care Programs for Children.* Proceedings of an institute jointly sponsored by the Tulane University School of Social Work and the Louisiana State Dept. of Health. New Orleans, Tulane University, April 8-12, 1957.

U. S. DEPT. OF HEALTH, EDUCATION, AND WELFARE, PUBLIC HEALTH Service. *Bibliography of World Literature on Mental Retardation,* January, 1940 - March, 1963.

——————: *Planning of Facilities for the Mentally Retarded.* Pub. No. 1181 B-1, November, 1964.

——————: *The President's Panel on Mental Retardation, Report of the Task Force on Prevention, Clinical Services and Residential Care, August,* 1962.

——————: *Report of the Mission to Denmark and Sweden,* 1963.

——————: *Report of the Mission to the Netherlands,* 1963.

——————: *Report of the Task Force on Education and Rehabilitation, August,* 1962.

U. S. DEPT. OF HEALTH, EDUCATION, AND WELFARE, THE PRESIDENT'S PANEL ON MENTAL RETARDATION: *Mental Retardation, A National Plan for a National Problem.* Washington, U. S. Government Printing Office, 1963.

U. S. DEPT. OF HEALTH, EDUCATION, AND WELFARE, OFFICE OF PROGRAM ANALYSIS: *Handbook on Programs of the U. S. Dept. of Health, Education, and Welfare.* 1963.

U. S. DEPT. OF HEALTH, EDUCATION, AND WELFARE: *New Directions in Health, Education and Welfare.* June, 1963.

——————: *The White House Conference on Mental Retardation: Proceedings.* 1963.

——————: *The Rehabilitated Mentally Retarded.* April, 1964.

U. S. DEPT. OF LABOR, OFFICE OF MANPOWER, AUTOMATION AND TRAINING: The mentally retarded: their special training needs. In *Manpower Research,* Bulletin No. 6, October, 1964.

VATH, WILLIAM R.: School for forgotten children. *Today's Health,* Vol. 39, July, 1961.

WARNER, W. LLOYD, MEEKER, MARCHIA, AND EELLS, KENNETH: *Social Class in America.* New York, Harper Torchbooks, 1960.

WASKOWITZ, CHARLOTTE H.: The parents of retarded children speak for themselves, *J Pediat, 54*:319, 1959.

WELLIN, EDWARD: "Public and Professional Attitudes Toward Mental Retardation." A presentation before the Public Health Nurses Section of the Forty-second Biennial Convention of the American Nurses' Association, Miami Beach, Florida, May 2-6, 1960.

WELLIN, EDWARD, *et al.*: Community aspects of mental subnormality— a local health department program for retarded children. *Amer J Public Health,* No. 1, Vol. 50, January, 1960.

WILLIE, CHARLES V.: The social class of patients that public health nurses prefer to serve. *Amer J Public Health,* Vol. 50, No. 8, August, 1960.

WORLD HEALTH ORGANIZATION: *The Mentally Subnormal Child.* World Health Organization Technical Report Series, No. 75, 1954.

WORTIS, JOSEPH: Towards the establishment of special clinics for retarded children. *Amer J Ment Defic,* No. 3, *58*:472-478, January, 1954.

————————: Mental retardation as a public health program. *Amer J Public Health,* No. 5, *45*:632-636, May, 1955.

YARROW, MARIAN RADKE, SCHWARTZ, CHARLOTTE GREEN, MURPHY, HARRIET S., AND DEASY, LEILA CALHOUN: The psychological meaning of mental illness in the family. *The Journal of Social Issues,* XI, No. 4, Vol. 11, 1955.

SWERLING, ISRAEL: Initial counseling of parents with mentally retarded children. *J Pediat,* No. 4, Vol. 44, April, 1954.

INDEX

A

Abnormalities
  anatomical or chemical, 3
  suspicion of, 37
  visual evidence of, 26
Action, a program of, 129
Adams, Richard, 75
Administration, clinic, xi, 7, 62
Administrator(s), 74
  clue to, 95
Administrative structures, 119
Adoption, child with multiple
  anomelies, 57
Adult activity center, short or long
  term, 124
Adult retardate
  goal for, 123
  productive member, 123
Adult retarded
  handicapped, 126
  productive, 126
  ongoing needs, 124, 126
Advice
  from friends, relatives, others, 9
  medical, 42, 43
  to parents, 5
Age
  of mother, 8
  variable, 6, 44
  when retardation recognized, 4
Agency
  community, 85
  federal, 98
Agencies, vocational rehabilitation, 105
Aggressiveness, 10
Albertson, Long Island, New York, 107
Analysis
  of data, 14

five major categories of, 32
  of interview, 67
Angell, Robert C., 118n
Anthropologist, 71, 72
Anxieties of parents, 5
Apathy, 10
Applicants, screening of, 108
Approach(es)
  coordinated, 101
  difference in philosophical, 12
  global, 97
  team, 12, 77
Aptekar, Herbert, 89
Association for the Help of Retarded
  Children, New York City, 122
Association of American Nurses, 71
Associations of parents, 125
Automation
  effect on retarded, 117
  unskilled problem, 117
Axelrod, Ida, xii

B

Beck, Helen, 89, 93n
Begab, Michael, 5n, 11, xvi, 89
Behavior of child, 4
  kinds of, 135
  leading to suspicion of mental
    retardation, 25, 32
Bell, Norman, 6n
Benda, Clemens E., 35, 36
Biases of staff, 70, 73, 76
Bigler, John A., 10n
Birth order, variable, 8
Blue-collar, 20, 45
Boggs, Elizabeth, 10n
Boston Association for Retarded

153